RELATIONSHIPS BETWEEN LOWLAND AND HIGHLAND PEOPLE OF CENTRAL AND SOUTH VIETNAM

A Historical Overview

DON VOTH

Order this book online at www.trafford.com
or email orders@trafford.com

Most Trafford titles are also available at major online book retailers.

Print information available on the last page.

ISBN: 978-1-6987-0077-9 (sc)
ISBN: 978-1-6987-0078-6 (e)

Library of Congress Control Number: 2020907266

Trafford rev. 04/22/2020

www.trafford.com
North America & international
toll-free: 1 888 232 4444 (USA & Canada)
fax: 812 355 4082

RELATIONSHIPS BETWEEN LOWLAND AND HIGHLAND PEOPLE

OF

CENTRAL AND SOUTH VIETNAM

A Historical Overview

Donald E. Voth[1]
Professor of Rural Sociology, Emeritus
University of Arkansas

---

[1] The author is currently Emeritus Professor of Rural Sociology at the University of Arkansas, having recently retired from appointment as Professor of Rural Sociology in teaching, research, and extension service. The mailing address is now 4323 Balcon Ct., NW, Albuquerque, NM, 87120. Most of the work reported here was performed while a graduate student in Southeast Asian Studies and Rural Sociology at Cornell University, 1966-1969, and immediately following while on the faculty in the Department of Community Development.at Southern Illinois University. The work was done in anticipation of doing field work on relationships between lowland Vietnamese society (Kinh) and the minorities of the Central Highlands, field work which was not possible because of the war. Other publications on this topic include Voth, Donald E. 1972. "Manipulating the Montagnards," Society, September/October, pp. 59-66; and "Translation from Nghiêm-Thẩm, Tìm Hiểu Đồng-Bào Thượng: Hai Phiền Vương cửa Triều Đình Việt-Nam hồi Trước, Thủy-Xá và Hoả-Xá (Seeking to Understand the Highland People: The Two Tribal Kingdoms of the Vietnamese Court in the Past, King of Fire and King of Water), Quê-Hương, Vol. 31 (January, 1962), pp. 130-150. Published in Southeast Asia: An International Quarterly, Vol. 1 (Fall), pp. 335-363.

CONTENTS

INTRODUCTION

This is an attempt at a preliminary assessment of an important but seriously neglected aspect of Vietnamese social history; inter-relationships between lowland and highland society. This problem was important on the Chinese frontier, in the Center, and in the South. I shall deal only with the problem in the Center and South, where relationships were with the Mon Khmer Austroasiatic peoples and the Cham-related Malayo-Polynesian peoples found in the highlands as far north as Quảng Bình and as far south as Biên Hoà. It is important to note that ethnically and linguistically these highland people are quite different from those in the North and along the Chinese frontier.[2]

I have divided the paper into four parts, dealing with three very general questions. First I examine the forces in traditional lowland society which were the driving force of the Nam Tiến (advance to the South) and which, consequently, created the groups and individuals who were on the frontier in contact with the highland societies. This force is the conflict between the central government and the village for control of the population and of agricultural resources. Unfortunately, this section is largely speculative as I have not been able to do the detailed historical research on local administration which would be required to fully substantiate this interpretation.

Secondly I consider the antiquity of formal relationships between the lowland court and the highland people, examining the claim that direct administration by the court began around 1540 and that tributary relationships with the "kings" of the Jarai began in 1558.

---

[2] Hoàng Xuân Hãn deals with the question of relationships with the highland people on the Chinese frontier during the Ly dynasty of the 11th to 13th centuries (Hoàng Xuân Hãn, 1966:100-101; 109-111). During this period of time and in this area, as he points out, intermarriage was frequently used by the Ly court to obtain alliances with highland groups. Ly princesses were offered in marriage to highland chiefs (Hoàng Xuân Hãn, 1966: 109-110). It is, perhaps, remarkable that this was never done on the Southern frontier with the highland people of the South.

Thirdly I examine the patterns and objectives of these relationships. This is really the core of the paper, and it suggests a number of tentative conclusions which should be the topic of more detailed historical research.

Finally there are presented conclusions drawn from the paper as a whole.

This does not pretend to be an exhaustive study of these inter-relationships. I have acquired a considerable amount of material on the subject which I analyze here in a preliminary fashion in order to stimulate interest and assist others more competent to deal with the historical questions involved. My sources are primarily the various published reports of the French explorers and administrators and Vietnamese court documents. The latter are not covered as thoroughly as I should like--and it is my conviction that there are important resources here which need to be exploited in analyzing relationships between highland and lowland people. Because the highland people were peripheral to the major concerns of the court, this will not be a easy task[3].

Probably the most useful initial source is Maitre (1912). Henri Maitre was one of the French explorers of the Central Highlands of Vietnam, and particularly of the Darlac plateau. He was assassinated there by dissident highlanders at Post Rolland in 1914, only two years after his book was written. In it (Les Jungles Moi, 1912) he recounts his exploration in the area and in Laos. The last chapter is his history of the highland people of the region and of their contact with the lowland Vietnamese and the Cham. This book was used extensively by Bourotte (1955), as well as by others who have written on the highland people of South Vietnam. Perhaps the most useful source for the accounts of other French explorers is the journal *Excursions et Reconnaissances*, which was published by the government of Cochinchina in Saigon at the end of the 19th century. Another useful item is *Varieties Sur Les Pays Mois*, also published by the government of Cochinchina. An essential source is the Phủ Man Tạp Lục (PMTL), *Notes on the Pacification of the Barbarians*, written in 1871 by Nguyễn Tấn (alias Nguyễn Ôn Khê), a mandarin who "pacified" the highland people of present day Quảng Ngãi, Quảng Nam and Bình

---

[3] Although they did receive more attention than most contemporary historical research indicates.

4

Định provinces between 1863 and 1869. It is available in Sino-Vietnamese in a private collection in Saigon, in the Toyo Bunko in Tokyo, and has recently been acquired from the Toyo Bunko by the library of Southern Illinois University.[4] It was published in Revue Indochinoise in a French translation in 1904 under the title "Phủ Man Tạp Lục, ou *Notes Diverses Sur La Pacification de la Region des Moi*." There are several important Vietnamese language sources, most of which are discussed in the important article by Nghiêm Thẩm (1962). I have used, in addition to translated excerpts from Nghiêm Thẩm's article, Auberet (1969), the Đại Nam Thục Lục, Nguyễn Siêu (1960), The Như Viễn from the Khâm Định Đại Nam Hội Điển Sự Lệ, Phan Huy Chú (1960, 1961), and the Đại Nam Nhất Thống Chí. Those which have proven the most useful are the Đại Nam Thục Lục (DNTL), which is the principal historical record of the Nguyễn dynasty, the Đại Nam Chính Biên Liệt Truyện (Nghiêm Thẩm, 1962) which has a special section on relationships with tributary states and barbarians. It is evident from the Đại Nam Thục Lục, for example, that the barbarians were of explicit concern to the court quite frequently and under varying circumstances. Indeed, one wonders to what degree Hoàng Xuân Hãn's assessment of the importance of the highland peoples on the Chinese frontier during the Ly dynasty (1010 to 1225) also applies in the South: "Below we shall see that all of the controversies between the Ly and the Sung resulted from the conflicts among the people of the highlands (dân khê động), either conflicts which arose among them or conflicts which were stimulated by the Ly court" (Hoàng Xuân Hãn, 1966:101).

---

[4] References to the present in the paper refer to the period when the paper was written, circa 1969-74.

THE NAM TIẾN (ADVANCE TO THE SOUTH) AND THE ORIGINS OF AGENTS OF CONTACT IN LOWLAND SOCIETY

One of the important questions in Vietnamese history is the cause of the Nam Tiến (advance to the South).[5] Was it "demographic pressure" (Lương Đức Thiệp, 1971:84), or an expansionist ideology, or a combination of both? What is meant by "demographic pressure?" As W. F. Wertheim has pointed out, this term must include, not only the numbers of people and the amount of land, but also the absorptive capacity of the relevant social and economic organization (Wertheim, 1965:202). This question of the origins of the Nam Tiến is directly relevant to the study of highland-lowland relationships in Vietnamese history because it, alone, can throw light upon the social origins of the lowlanders who were found on the frontier, and under what circumstances, vis-a-vis the society of their origins, they found themselves. Implicit in this statement is the fact that the frontier itself and its role in Vietnamese history should receive more attention than they have in the past.[6]

There were, essentially, three categories or classes of lowland people on the frontiers of Vietnamese society. The first was the Vietnamese underclass or rural proletariat. This class was made up of a melange of disenfranchised peasants, vagabonds, bandits, erstwhile criminals, with these categories not necessarily being mutually exclusive. I shall be primarily concerned with the origins of this group. The second group was much smaller than the first. It was made up of legitimate officials, both military and civilian, who were found on the frontier. Although I do not examine this group in detail, there is some discussion of it and its origins. The third group is also smaller than the first. It is made up of political exiles, agitators, and rebels. The Vietnamese frontier has always been a potential haven for individuals or groups who were in conflict with the

---

[5] The journal Sử Địa recently devoted an entire issue to the Nam Tiến. By the editors own admission, it is only a beginning in a fascinating story (Sử Địa 1970:19-20). See also Cotter (1986).

[6] But see Hoàng Xuân Hãn's comment, as well as McAlister (Hoàng Xuân Hãn, 1966:101; McAlister, 1967:771-844).

ruling dynasty, and in this sense the frontier has always had considerable political significance. This group is not analyzed in its own right in this paper, although it is mentioned several times.

Although the subject is not dealt with in this paper, it is interesting to speculate on the degree to which these three groups were inter-related. For example, to what extent were legitimate officials recruited from the first group?[7]

Much has been made of the village as the basic unit of Vietnamese society, as the major point of reference for behavior of the Vietnamese people, and of its humanistic and democratic characteristics (McAlister, 1969:32-35; Mus, 1952:23-35; 1949). The importance of the village and its uniqueness has, of course, been illustrated time and again by the famous adage, "The customs of the village have precedence over the laws of the king" (Lệ Vua Thưa Lệ Làng.) Like all proverbs, it seems to me this one is more important in the issue which it underlines than in the specific solution it suggests, not that there is not some truth to the latter as well, as we shall see presently. For the present at least, the important issue is that there is, throughout Vietnamese history, a conflict between the central government and the village. I shall try to show that this conflict, itself, resulted in a centrifugal society, a characteristic which was facilitated by specific institutional means, and that from these centrifugal tendencies there resulted a sizable group of lowland people who tried to find refuge on the frontiers. Briffaut states the thesis well:

> But the forests and mountains were not only the domain of retarded highlanders and Annamites, those whom the teachings of the court had not reached. They also served as a refuge for a virtual floating population which originated directly from the sedentary villages.
>
> These were people who had fled because of some calamity, citizens who were uprooted by war or by natural disasters. They fled en masse in a sad exodus, seeking a better fatherland and a more beneficent god. They did not became established upon new lands, hopeless as they were in the middle of uncultivated lands, they wandered and sought adventure. The crowd which had lost its City and its God simply dispersed (Briffaut, 1912:Vol. 3:20). (My translation)

---

[7] See, for example, the instance in Thuận Khánh (Now Bình Thuận), and Khánh Hòa where a mandarin recommended that an ex-convict who know the local customs and languages of the man (barbarians) be selected as the commercial agent. His suggestion was approved by the court (DNTL, Vol. 17:174).

In a social system that depends entirely upon the resources of the soil which are exploited with a minimum of specialization, those individuals or political entities which control the land tend to have the dominant position. In Vietnam, this dominance can be judged by the effective control of private lands, the effective control of communal lands, effective fiscal policy, and such things as the maintenance of peace and public works. In general, the periods when the central government exercised effective control over land, private and communal, seem to have been periods of peace, periods when banditry was minimized, periods when the public works were maintained, but also periods when the local village elites were the most strictly regulated, to the benefit, at least from the official point of view, of the masses of the population. It is this control of the conditions of livelihood of the peasants which was the object of a struggle between the state or the centralized power and the local elites, referred to by the French as the "notables". These notables were village leaders who held positions of leadership because of economic status and perhaps also because of kinship and education.

An Overview of the History of Village Autonomy

Apparently in the 13th century the Lý dynasty consolidated its political control by establishing a feudal system which resulted in fiscal distress and hardship for the people (Vũ Văn Hiền, 1939:23; Buttinger, 1956:146, 147). In 1397 and 1398 the response to this was limiting the size of land holdings to 10 mẫu (0.36 hectare equals one Tonkinese mẫu) for anyone who was not of royal blood and the establishment of a census. The most celebrated reforms of this early period, however, are associated with the Lê dynasty after the defeat of the Minh overlords in 1428 (Vũ Văn Hiền, 1939:24-30; Nguyễn Hữu Khang, 1946:35, 36; Lê Thành Khôi, 1955: 217,220). These reforms mark the high-water point in the degree to which the state controlled resources at the expense of village elites. Again, they were associated with the fiscal demands of the state as well as with the need to ameliorate poverty. According to Vũ Văn Hiền:

> It was necessary to come to the assistance of the poor inhabitants who had
> not a single piece of land upon which to establish themselves, and many of whom
> had rendered service to the country in going into combat. It was also necessary to

stabilize the rural communities, since the communal land taxes, and especially the head taxes of the registered villagers, furnished the regular revenues for the public treasury. These objectives, at the same time fiscal, social, and political, were never separated. They inspired the reforms of Lê Thái Tổ and his successors during the fifteenth century, which consisted on the one hand of a general distribution of land and on the other of the establishment of the legal status of the communal lands. All of the inhabitants were beneficiaries of the general distribution of lands which occurred shortly after the general census of the population and of cultivable land in 1428 and 1429. From the highest dignitaries to the poor, orphans, isolated persons (widows and widowers), boys and girls, every- one received his share. (Vũ Văn Hiền, 1939:24) (My translation).

Thus these reforms established and regulated communal lands and encouraged the exploitation of new lands. Communal lands were to be distributed periodically and the distribution was to be determined by the social rank of each individual. Communal lands could not be sold and any contract to the contrary was nullified by the state (Vũ Văn Hiền, 1939:27; Lê Thành Khôi, 1955:220-225; Nguyễn Hữu Khang, 1946:38). They could not be transmitted by inheritance. The formation of large land holdings was forbidden. Taxes were drawn from the communal lands and from the head tax, therefore to leave one's parcel of communal land unexploited was to invite seizure and redistribution. The essential characteristic of these reforms is that the central government injected itself into local village affairs, regulating the disposition of communal lands, etc. In fact, it intervened to the point of carrying out a census of population and of arable land in 1428 and 1429, something that was never to be done again until during the French administration in the 1930's. However, in 1461 Lê Thánh Tông provided for the election of village officials rather than their appointment by the court. This, no doubt, was very significant in the subsequent development of village autonomy. In any case, the court's ability to intervene in internal affairs of the village seems never again to have been as extensive as it was during the 15th century.[8]

---

[8] The historical development of the village-center conflict has been interpreted in several different ways. Nguyễn Hữu Khang, whose interpretation is most closely followed in this paper, held that village autonomy increased when the central government was weak. Nguyễn Xuân Đạo has pointed out, however, that villages were given the right to elect their own officials

In the 17th century the military demands of a civil war strained the resources of the system. No doubt recognizing the efficiency of the local authorities, the state concentrated its growing demands upon the village as a unit through these authorities rather than dealing directly with individuals or families. In 1662 Lê Thánh Tông required village authorities to be responsible for the head tax and thus contact of the state with individuals was lost (Nguyễn Hữu Khang, 1946:42; Vũ Văn Hiền, 1939:32). In 1660 a census was attempted but it was unsuccessful, perhaps this was the reason for the change in 1662. Then, in 1730 when the court attempted to get an accurate census, the notables threatened to revolt and the proposed census was not carried out (Nguyễn Hữu Khang, 1946:43).

The ensuing period of turmoil no doubt strengthened the position of the village elites. Governmental control over them was non-existent or very weak. Their position was even more directly enhanced by peasants who, instead of becoming brigands, merely had their name removed from the village list, thus forfeiting their rights to communal land, and employed themselves to the local landholders. The same process made land available for purchase by the landholders. Regarding this period Vu Van Hien says: ". . . a part of the population. . . lived from day to day by begging and stealing." (Vũ Văn Hiền, 1939:31; Lê Thành Khôi, 1955:258).[9]

The reforms of the 17th and 18th centuries were attempts to reinstate the static hierarchical division of agricultural resources of the Lê in the 15th century and appealed to by Confucian scholars. The most important innovations were the exclusion of landholders from the distribution of communal lands on the one hand and further sanctioning their actual control over agrarian and fiscal affairs in the village on the other. Since 1662, when the state effectively lost

---

during a period when the central government was strong (Nguyễn Xuân Đạo, 1960:15). I do not believe that this one instance necessarily negates the existence of a general trend. In any case, it is the village-center conflict per se rather than its precise historical development which is significant. See Phạm Thế Hùng for an excellent overview of village government in Vietnam (Phạm Thế Hùng, 1972). Hùng also sees village autonomy developing gradually since approximately the 15th century.

[9] Khôi proposes a cyclical process of feudal oppression, popular revolt, and agrarian reform (Lê Thành Khôi, 1955:258).

its control over individuals, this process was never stopped and it always tended to invalidate other reforms. Extraordinary personal taxes were created in 1722 and 1742 and property taxes were increased in 1722, 1728, 1740, and 1756 (Deloustal, 1910:461). The situation became so serious that a Trinh prince proposed a general collectivization of all land in 1740, a proposal which was not, however, accepted. The following quotations illustrate the degree to which the situation had deteriorated by the end of the 18th century:

> Then, from numerous indications, one can sense that the structure of government began to fall apart. The grave troubles which weakened the central power caused it to gradually relax its supervision of the villages. In the villages local customs developed in violation of the law. These customs became important for resisting or opposing the application of royal ordinances. At the same time the village chiefs, previously appointed by the mandarins, gradually began to be selected by the inhabitants themselves.
>
> This became habitual during the reigns of Long Đức (1723-1734) and Vĩnh Hựu (1735-1740). This evolution is very important. Thereafter the village came to possess a high degree (almost complete) of autonomy. It became a state within a state, having its own patrimony, its own laws, and its own administration. (Khang. 1946:48) (My translation).
>
> But towards the end of the century, the situation became worse and gradually before the arrival of the armies of Gia Long, the founder of the Nguyễn dynasty, the Tonkinese countryside went into an era of constant insecurity because of the presence of a mass of vagabonds during consecutive years of drought and periods of misery resulting from floods and epidemics. (Vũ Văn Hiền. 1939:35) (My translation)

Gia Long (1802-1819) emphasized agrarian affairs during the time that he was fighting the Tây Sơn rebels but when he established the Nguyễn dynasty over the whole country his interest, and that of his successors, was primarily in the center of Vietnam (the reform of Minh Mạng in 1839) (Nguyễn Thiệu Lâu. 1951: 119) and in the exploitation of more land for an enlarged tax base (Vũ Văn Hiền, 1939:38). Apparently the reforms of Minh Mạng were not successful, although in theory they were worked out quite carefully (Gaultier. 1935:259; Nguyễn Văn Thái and Nguyễn Văn Mùng. 1958: 239). The new code of Gia Long did make some changes in the administration of communal lands but they are hardly worth discussing because they were not realized in practice (Vũ Văn Hiền, 1939: 41-43; Buttinger, 1956: 282. 315). Under threat from the French, Tự Đức finally had to revert to the selling of communal lands in order to finance his army (Nguyễn Thiệu Lâu. 1951:119).

Thus, the situation immediately prior to the arrival of the French was one of a weak state, unable to resist the growing independence of the local villages and unable to manipulate any aspect of the life of the peasants in a manner favorable to the development of support, political or fiscal, of the central government by the peasants.[10]

There are three areas which need to be considered during the French period: local administration, legal developments, and economic developments. They are too complicated to set forth in detail so this will, again, be a mere overview. Administratively, power was first removed from village elites. However, this was evidently not successful, and when the French realized it was failing they proceeded more gradually. They did not reach a point of very extensive centralized control of village affairs until very late during the French period.[11] Vũ Văn Hiền emphasizes that, legally, by 1935 the French administration had succeeded in enforcing aspects of the traditional land policy much more successfully than the Vietnamese emperors had been able to do for hundreds of years (Vũ Văn Hiền, 1939:68; Boudillon, 1915). A significant difference was that land ownership was stabilized since it was not under threat of seizure and eventually the country was pacified so that the fluctuations in the influence of the central government no longer existed to a significant degree (Vũ Văn Hiền, 1939:48; Goudal,

---

[10] See also Nguyễn Xuân Đạo (1960), Roy Jumper (1962) , and Phạm Thế Hùng (1972) for treatments of local government.

[11] See also Nguyễn Xuân Đạo (1960). The collection of civil status data, the survey of communal lands, and the regulation of village budgets had begun in 1883. It was only in 1904 that an arrete was passed that seriously limited the administrative powers of the traditional notables. This appeared to be unsuccessful because the local elites withdrew completely and village affairs fell into the hands of people who were incompetent. In 1927 this was revised with the result that the notables, although they were selected by the village, were subject to approval by the province chief. Above the village level local representation was almost non-existent. The last reforms of 1944 attempted to centralize the choice of notables even more.

1938:188). One of the results of this was a resettlement of populations back to rural areas,

coming in from both north and south. A good example of this process is the history of the

resettlement of the province of Thanh Hoá given by Robequain (Robequain, 1929:Vol. 2:292).

The most important legal effects of the French administration were more explicit statement of

the policies of ancient Vietnam, enforcement, and providing means of litigation. In the economic

sphere, in spite of the fact that legal regulations somewhat restricted their misuse of communal

lands, the power of local elites was probably increased. This is a distinct change from the pre-

French period, when the strength of the central government was negatively correlated with the

strength of village elites. This is because French economic policies differed drastically from

those of the Vietnamese dynasties. Regularization of legal matters, enforcement, and

pacification freed village elites from the threat of seizure or robbery (Cadiere, 1912:60). The

most important means of strengthening these elements was, however, programs for the extension

of agricultural credit which were supposed to help poor peasants but which, on the contrary, did

more to strengthen people who already had some means.[12] This does not mean, as Ellen

Hammer supposed, that the French administration disrupted a peaceful and successful village

system; it means, rather, that they regulated its environment and allowed it to realize its logical

conclusion (Hammer, 1954:62). The evidence of economic control of the land by local elites is

plentiful but it is discussed most carefully by Gourou (1940) and Robequain (1944) (See also

Jacoby, 1949; Yves Henry, 1932; and USDA, 1950). Pierre Pasquier, Governor General of

Indochina, is quoted as follows:

> If only the loans had been granted directly to the needy nhà quê or the
> poverty stricken ta điền! The depressing fact is that the credit facilities so far
> granted have had no psychological or economic effects. It has indeed proved
> almost impossible to bring these advances within the reach of the small farmer,
> the ta điền, or the nhà quê, except through the large or medium scale landowners.
> . .all the efforts made by my administrative officers to improve the situation of
> these poor people are therefore brought to naught; any attempt to lower the cost of
> production of rice by reducing the interest of loans is doomed to failure in

---

[12] See Gourou (1940:231,429), Robequain (1929:Vol. 2:268), Goudal (1938:210-215) for French
programs in agricultural credit.

advance. The large and medium-scale landowners charge a tremendous commission equal to the difference between the interest charged on loans by the rural funds and the rates at which they lend money directly or which they charge for standing security. Their maleficent influence prevents any direct contact between the authorities and the rural masses.[13]

The report of a study done by the ILO in 1938 claimed the existence of two classes in all of the Vietnamese countryside; the large and medium sized landholders who benefit from the economic developments and who do not engage in manual labor on the one hand, and the small-holders, tenant farmers, share tenants, and agricultural wage workers, all of whom are more less subject to the other group on the other (Goudal, 1938:193; Dumarest, 1935).

Taking as his basis the study done by Yves Henry (1932), which discovered that small holders (less than 1.8 hectares) occupied 36.6% of the land, medium holders (1.8 to 3.6 hectares) 26.6%[14] of the land, and large holders (3.6 hectares and more) 16.6% of the land in Tonkin, Gourou discussed what he believed to be the real situation, which was much worse than these figures suggest. Part of the reason for this was the unfortunate choice of categories by Henry. Gourou felt that small holders should have been designated as those who had up to 3 mẫu (1.08 hectares) instead of 5 mẫu (1.8 hectares).

> The delta is certainly essentially a district of smallholders, but their exact proportion is far from clear. There can be practically no doubt that large holdings are very rare, and that medium-sized holdings which enable the proprietors to live in comfort without doing any manual work are of ridiculously small area to our way of thinking (a few hectares, or even one hectare only); in addition there are swarms of tiny holdings of a few thousand or even a few hundred square meters...but these general truths require to be confirmed by material evidence. It must be borne in mind that the apparent proprietor is not always the real one; the owner may have made over his land to a money-lender, who allows him to remain

---

[13] Pierre Pasquier, quoted in Jacoby (1949:150, 151). This is a lament now depressingly familiar to Westerners engaged in economic development efforts premised upon a "trickle down" theory of how development occurs.

[14] There appears to be an error in Gourou's figures here. He states that medium holders have from 1.8 to 5.6 hectares or from 5 to 10 mau. At 0.36 hectares per mau he must have meant 1.8 to 3.6 hectares.

on the holding in return for an annual payment; he appears to be a landowner but he is really only a tenant. Thus, openly or secretly, large holdings are acquired; the rates of interest are high and inevitably favour the expropriation of smallholders, who find themselves obliged to borrow . . . the free play of economic forces naturally leads to the expropriation of the owners of small properties. (Goudal, 1938:191, translated by him from Gourou, 1936: 117, 118).[15]

It is the delta region where large landholdings have developed the most. In Thái Bình an official investigation showed that 122,000 proprietors of more than one mẫu possessed, altogether, 61,000 mẫu whereas 253 proprietors of large holdings owned outright 28,000 mẫu and controlled another 43,000 mẫu which, although they appeared to belong to the original owners on the land records, had actually been alienated, leaving the original owners as tenants on latifundia. (Gourou, 1940:230)[16] (My translation)

In his summary Mr. Gourou makes the point that, in of the relative absence of the kind of large holdings to be found in Cochinchina, the solidarity of the Northern village makes the hierarchical arrangement even more effective and even more difficult to combat (Gourou, 1940:428). The evidence, admittedly, is somewhat superficial. The data needed to indicate the precise nature of the concentration of power in traditional Vietnamese village systems is not available, partially because of the resistance that the village had developed to intervention from the outside. The evidence does suggest that power was significantly concentrated and that relationships which would be regarded as exploitative did exist. This system was not to be easily broken down by the French administration nor was it open to inquiry about the degree to which inequalities actually existed.[17]

---

[15] Goudal quotes figures from Gourou (1936:117, 118).

[16] Goudal (1938:190-191) classifies peasants into very poor peasants (no land or fractions of a hectare), small holders (1 to 2 hectares), medium sized farmers (7 to 18 hectares), and tenant and share farmers. This is very similar to the classifications used by the Democratic Republic of Vietnam (North) in their land reform in the 1950's.

[17] For the opinion of a French official on the duplicity of local officials see Emile Delamarre (1924:200).

Thus, I conclude that the Vietnamese village in the North was a relatively closed system in which power was concentrated in those who exercised effective control over the conditions of existence for the rest of the population--the land and the influence of the state. There is no justification for calling this system a democracy in the normal sense of the term.[18] As would be expected, a great amount of conflict arose at the point of contact between the village and the central government involving, of course, local village officials since they represented the village to the outside (Delamarre, 1924). This conflict was very fluid from time to time.

One of the direct consequences of this contest between the center and the villages was the Nam Tiến. When the central government was strong the country was pacified, public works were maintained, and village elites were at least partially controlled by the state. When the central government was weak village elites gained ascendancy under circumstances of general insecurity, brigandage, etc. Apparently there were significant fluctuations in the relative power of the state, leading to the cyclical interpretation of Vietnamese history (Lê Thành Khôi 1955:258).

The Creation of Vagabonds by the Village-Center Conflict

What emerges here is an on-going contest between the central government and the village authorities for control of certain essential aspects of the peasants' subsistence base, primarily land. Normally, the central government tended toward socialistic and egalitarian types of solutions; redistribution of communal lands, restrictions upon the size of private holdings, etc. The villages, on the other hand, tended toward feudalism. The central government, however, always depended upon village officials to administer reforms as well as normal fiscal and legal matters. Consequently, the central government was forced to use the village as the basis for defining citizenship. Briffaut has detailed the restrictions upon residence and movement, all of

---

[18] "Elle n'est démocratique qu'en apparence, et le principe du suffrage universel n'y a pas encore d'application; pratiquement, les pauvres sent exclus des deliberations, et, si les viellards sent honores et consultes, c'est une petite oligarchie des gens riches ou pourvus de grades mandarinaux--nous dirons de capacitaires--qui prend les decisions essentielles (Robequain, 1929:Vol. 2:212).

which resulted in "legitimate" citizenship being defined as membership in a village (Briffaut, 1912). Legitimate villagers, those known to the central government, were those registered in the civil register, the Đinh Bộ. However, it was well known, both to the Vietnamese court as well as to the French administration, that the civil register included only a fraction of the actual village population. This is why nationwide censuses were attempted, and it is also the reason why they were so vehemently opposed by village elites. There existed, in addition to those on the civil register, a virtual rural proletariat who attached themselves to villages as landless agricultural laborers. These people were classified by Vũ Văn Hiền as the dân lậu (the "uncontrolled," those in violation of the law, or Briffaut's "errants"). Two other categories of non-registered residents were the dân ngoại (strangers, presumably staying only temporarily), and ngũ cư (temporary residents). He claims that in 1884 only one-third of those who should be on the village registers actually were on them (Vũ Văn Hiền, 1939:89). Nguyễn Cư Trình, in 1751, referred to two categories of dân lậu, those who simply evaded taxes and those who were too poor to pay taxes.

> There are two categories of dân lậu, those who evade (trốn) taxes and who become vagabonds (đi lang thang), and those who move because they are poor. Now, if we do not discriminate, but put them all on the list for tax collection, they will disperse, hiding themselves in the jungle. Surely the village residents should not be penalized for them. Let us investigate those who evade taxes and determine which of them are able to make a living, and tax those as usual. As for those who are poor and hungry, let us exempt them from taxes and try to sustain them. The people must be treated in such a way that they will be peaceful, they must not be agitated, because if they are they are likely to rebel. If they are peaceful they are more easy to administer. (DNTL, Vol. 12:272) (My translation)

Briffaut quotes Trần Bá Lộc to the effect that there were three categories of dân lậu:

> There are three categories of poor people. Those of the first category are good, know good from evil, and when they are in debt seek the means to pay their debts and to support their families. Those of the second category work very little, associate with robbers and pirates, they never pay their debts and are always engaged in deceit. The third category do nothing, abandon themselves to stealing and idleness, take part in revolts, smoke opium, and obey not a single law. (Briffaut, 1912:Vol. 3:21) (My translation)

It was in the interest of local village elites to retain the illegal and undefined status of the rural proletariat.[19] First, the smaller the number of registered residents, the smaller the village tax, corvee labor requirement, and military assessment. Secondly, those who were not on the village register were not eligible for communal lands; consequently, the elites need not distribute these lands as extensively. Finally, the labor requirements of the intensive farming practiced by lowland Vietnamese were irregular and very great at certain periods of the year. The data presented by Henry indicate that the system must have required a supply of at least partially migratory agricultural labor (Henry, 1932:33; Robequain, 1944:74).

Since they were not in the village register, these agricultural laborers benefited little from the much vaunted welfare characteristics of the traditional Vietnamese village, as long as the central government had to depend so heavily upon the village elites to administer national policy there was no hope for reform. As is indicated by the quote from Pasquier above (page 13), the French administrators met the same impasse and had the same results.

The process whereby a villager could become a dân lậu is implicit in Nguyễn Cử Trình's quotation above (page 15) and is suggested by Goudal:

---

[19] See especially Briffaut on this point. "La cite a interet a adopter definitivement le plus grand nombre possible de ses stagiaires: ainsi grandit en population stable et en puissance economique; ainsi elle repare automatiquement les vides que les guerres, les epidemies. l'exode ou la loi penale ont creuses parmi les sedentaires; les stagiaires prennent alors la place des disparus. Cependant la cite a par contre interet a reculer le plus possible la date de l'agrement definitif des stagiaires,--ils sont taillables et corveables a merci--et a dissimuler leur existence au fisc imperial, en omettant de les coucher au role special; ils sont alors une source de profits illicites pour la commune.

Mais l'Empire n'a point de moyens de controle en ce qui concerns la classe plus speciale des errants: l'errant etait hier sans attache et sans famille, et le fisc ignorait son existence alors qu'il vagabondait; aujourd'hui qu'il est a l'ecole d'une cite, sa presence est dissimulee par la cite elle-meme dans quelque but interesse, et son nom n'est point couche sur le role special. C'est une unjustice et une fraude, presque sans recours" (Briffaut, 1912:Vol. 3:74-75).
Briffaut's "stagiaire" derives from his thesis that vagabonds could attach themselves to a village where they would be, literally, rehabilitated. During this time their status was probationary and, indeed, they had no formal status in the village at all.

The very poor peasant possesses nothing but a few ares of rice fields, scanty equipment for tilling the land, a pig, a few poultry and no savings of any kind. He works the land with his family, hires out his labour to neighboring land-owners and works as a wage earner during the agricultural slack season. To him and his family rice is a luxury, which enters into their diet only immediately after the harvest; for the rest of the year they are underfed. In a bad year he has to borrow in order to buy food, and once he has got into debt he is soon ruined {Goudal, 1938:190).

When he, thus, became indebted he would lose his lands, if he had any, and be unable to pay taxes, and eventually simply have to leave the village to escape the obligations which he could not meet. Once he left the village I doubt that, in everyday practice, anyone tried to distinguish between those who had done so legitimately and those who were principally interested in evading taxes. In a word, he became a vagabond, which was illegal, and hence, criminal.

These, then, were the populations who were responsible for Nam Tiến. Briffaut said of them:

The sedentary populations would be unjust to the errant if they would give him no hope because they owe much to him. They owe him the clearing and exploitation of the savage country, the progressive extension of the frontiers, the initial conquest of new lands, and, finally, the social education and pacification of the savages. (Briffaut. 1912: Vol. 3:30) (My translation)

In spite of the fact that contact with the barbarians of the highlands was forbidden for everyone except the enfranchised commercial agents who were, themselves, frequently refugees from sedentary villages, there is ample evidence that it was quite frequent (Hickey, 1958:42-43; Aymonier, 1885:250, 273, 224; Maitre, 1912: 474; Neiss, 1935:30; Verneville, 1882:287-289; Humann, 1935:106-107; Nyo, 1937:56; Gautier, 1935:46; Bourotte, 1955:85). Briffaut would have us believe that contact was forbidden because of a fear of "contamination des moeurs" (Briffaut, 1912:Vol. 3:12). No doubt there was some truth to this. However, there are at least two other compelling, and much simpler reasons. The first was that the court was vitally interested in preserving the trade in valuable forest products of the frontier for itself, and it knew very well that lowlanders settling in the highlands would find the temptation to carry on trade themselves too strong to resist. The second reason is well illustrated in Briffaut's own paraphrasing of the Gia Long Code, Article 224:

> ...whoever has fled to the islands of the sea, to the deep valleys of the savages, to the dense forests of the barbarians, territories which have not benefited from the educative influence of the king, it often happens that such criminals gather crowds of people to themselves and raise fortifications for military defense. (Briffaut, 1912:VoI 3:19, from Gia Long Code, Art. 224) (my translation).

In a word, the court was acutely aware of the possibility that these disenfranchised peasants, who, in spite of their delicate legal status, still aspired to the values of sedentary village life, might use the highland frontier as a base from which to attack lowland villages.

Institutional Arrangements Which Promoted Going to the Frontier

The Vietnamese court had two policies which greatly facilitated the Nam Tiến. The first and most important, especially after Gia Long defeated the Tây Sơn in 1802, was land development colonies. These were referred to as Dinh Điền and Đồn Điền. The former were "civilian" colonies and the latter "military" colonies. The second policy of significance was the use of exile as a punishment for crimes.

Colonization

Colonization appears frequently in Vietnamese history. In the period immediately after 1470 peasants from the north were sent to colonize the lands newly taken from the Charn, and during this time, one may infer, the contact between lowland people and southern highland people began. When Prince Nguyễn Hoàng was appointed governor of the southern provinces in 1558, one of the things he was charged with was colonizing the arca (Cadiere, 1906; Cotter, 1968). After the defeat of the Tây Sơn, the Nguyễn dynasty made extensive use of these colonies to clear and exploit the land in the South.

Although, as Briffaut points out, vagabonds from the Vietnamese underclass could be reincorporated into existing villages by attaching themselves to landowners as tenants, or to the village itself to supply whatever labor requirements the village might have such as corvee or military service (Briffaut, 1912:Vol. 3:66), perhaps the most significant means of being rehabilitated was by joining one of the colonies on the frontier, settling down, and eventually beginning to pay taxes again. During the Nguyễn dynasty vagabonds were enlisted to join such settlements (Lương Đức Thiệp, 1971:84; Aubaret, 1969: 2, ll; Briffaut, 1912:Vol. 3:30). Tự Đức decreed that anyone who enlisted vagabonds to clear land on the frontier would be rewarded by being exempted from corvee and military service, and anyone who cleared 20 mẫu (approximately 0.36 hectare) and enlisted ten people eligible for taxation could request the establishment of a new village (Lương Đức Thiệp, 1971:105, 106).[20]

The difference between the military colonies and the civilian colonies apparently was that the former were populated by soldiers, prisoners of war, or criminals, and administered by military officials, whereas the latter were administered by civilian officials. The land in these settlements eventually belonged to the individual settlers, and they, "were usually given a three-year grace period before they were required to pay taxes." (Lương Đức Thiệp, 1971:106).

Tự Đức also decreed that criminals who could, within a period of three years, clear at least three mẫu, would be pardoned of their crimes (Lương Đức Thiệp, 1971: 106).

Of course, it appears that in many areas of the South, lowland settlers more or less drifted in on their own initiative, only to be followed later by the schemes of the court to organize them into colonies or regular villages (Trần Trọng Kim, 1964:329).[21]

Exile as a Part of the Criminal Justice System

It was customary as punishment for certain crimes to send convicts into exile on the frontiers. According to Lương Đức Thiệp, during the Nguyễn dynasty, crimes were punished, in order of gravity by the rattan whip in five degrees from ten to fifty strokes, the cane whip in five

---

[20] See Lương Đức Thiệp (1971 :105-106) for the criteria involved. Excluded, for example, were small children and women.

[21] In this case the effects of the Trịnh-Nguyễn wars apparently caused many people to go to the Đồng Nai area and to Bà Rịa to settle. See also Nguyễn Văn Hầu (1970: 11).

degrees from sixty to one hundred strokes, hard labor in three degrees from one to three years, exile consisting of three degrees from 200 to 300 dặm away from one's home, and, finally, death in two degrees, including hanging and decapitation. If exile was for life, the convict took his family, as well as any agricultural implements and animals, with him in order to clear the land and farm (Lương Đức Thiệp, 1971:123- 124). These were persons who might populate the military colonies. Not surprisingly, convicts were fertile soil for potential rebels against the central government. The famous rebellion of Lê Văn Duyệt's adopted son, Lê Văn Khôi, began when he, with 27 convicts from Bắc Ky who were exiled to the South, rebelled (Trần Trọng Kim, 1964:445-446).

Exile as a form of punishment was finally abolished in 1887 under Đồng Khánh, apparently because the French opposed it (Briffaut, Vol. 1:165).

Thus it was these processes and institutions which provided the manpower for the Nam Tiến. The conflict between the central government and the village had the effect of generating a disenfranchised, rural proletariat, members of which frequently found the frontier an escape from the demands placed upon them. The land settlement villages on the frontier, exile as a penalty for criminals, and the various inducements for land development, all facilitated this movement. These, then, were the lowland Vietnamese most likely to confront the various minority groups during the Nam Tiến.

THE ANTIQUITY OF RELATIONSHIPS BETWEEN LOWLAND AND HIGHLAND PEOPLE

The antiquity of relationships between Vietnamese lowland society and the people of the Southern Highlands would seem to be well established. Maitre cites 1540 and 1558 as important landmarks, the first marking the naming of Bùi Tá Hán as the first Vietnamese governor of Quảng Nam[22] (Maitre, 1912:444), and the latter marking the recognition by the Jarai King of Fire

---

[22] This includes the area of the present provinces of Quảng Nam and Quảng Ngãi.

22

and King of Water of Vietnamese suzerainty (Maitre, 1912:448). One or the other or both of these dates have been used repeatedly to mark the beginning of these contacts (Bourotte, 1955:23; Nghiêm Thẩm, 1962:8; Nyo, 1937:30; Bùi Đình, 1963:86; Paul Nur, 1966:38, 56). Lê Ngọc Trụ and Phạm Văn Luật suggest that the Đa Vách and Trà Bông highland people recognized Vietnamese suzerainty "after 1470." (Lê Ngọc Trụ and Phạm Văn Luật, 1951:37) However, it is difficult to assess the validity of these statements. Of course, 1558 is an important date in Vietnamese history, marking the removal of Nguyễn Hoàng to the South (Thuận Hoá) eventually to establish the Nguyễn dynasty. It is not unreasonable to suppose that contacts with the Jarai of the high plateau may have been initiated at approximately that time. In the absence of specific evidence it seems unlikely, however, that 1558 was the exact year when these relationships began.

These dates do correspond, however, with two rather different patterns of relationships between lowland and highland societies. On the one hand there were highland people on the frontiers who were quite accessible, with whom there was direct competition for land, and who eventually became subordinated to the lowland administration. These were referred to locally as "Mọi Thuộc" (subordinate barbarians) in Quảng Nam (Durand, 1900:290-292) and as "annexed" people by Briffaut (Briffaut, 1912:Vol. 3:7), or, alternatively as "pacified" highland people. On the other hand, there were those who were distant, referred to as "Mọi Cao" (the highland barbarians) in Quảng Nam (Durand, 1900:290-292), but including, also, tributary groups, with whom there was no direct competition for land but who could be beneficial to the court through trade, through the prestige accorded the court by having numerous vassal states, and by helping to maintain peace on the frontiers. Fifteen forty is important in that it marks the beginning of the direct administration of highland people in one area, whereas 1558 is important in that it allegedly marks the beginning of tributary relationships with a remote and distant highland group in another area. The remaining discussion of the antiquity of the relationships with the people of the Southern Highlands will be organized according to these two types of relationships.

The Direct Administration of Highland People in Quảng Nam, Quảng Ngãi, and Bình Định.

A special administrative apparatus for highland people was created in the inland areas of the present Quảng Nam, Quảng Ngãi, and Bình Định provinces. No doubt there was precedent in the North for such a structure among the Thổ, Mán, and Thái groups (McAlister, 1967: 777-789; Hickey, 1958:106, 142-143), but I shall not deal with these precedents here. In Quảng Nam, Quảng Ngãi, and Bình Định the structure was referred to as the Trấn Man or the Sơn Phòng[23], the former term having been coined by Gia Long in 1804, and the latter by Tự Đức in 1863. Henri Maitre presented it as the basic paradigm of highland administration further South, throughout the Nam Tiến. This is not the place to present its details, or to judge this opinion of Maitre. Nevertheless, there is no doubt that it was a significant milestone and continuing experiment in relationships between the court and highland people who were most accessible and, consequently, an immediate administrative problem for lowland officials.

The basic question, then, is when this structure emerged and in what form it emerged first. There is, of course, no argument with dating Bùi Tá Hán's appointment as governor of Quảng Nam at 1540. The issue concerns the nature of his relationship with the highland people of the area. The only source of information on this question which I have been able to find and the one cited by Maitre, who was the source for all subsequent writers on highland history, is the Phủ Man Tạp Lục. Nguyễn Tấn, the author of this document, had just completed his task of "pacifying" the highland people of the area in 1869 when he wrote the Phủ Man Tạp Lục (PMTL) in 1871 as a private, family record. He gives very interesting details about his own campaign, about the life of the "barbarians" and about the administrative structure created to administer them. It also provides several brief historical sketches of the province, unfortunately without identifying any sources and with very little precision in the chronology of events portrayed. In any case, I shall quote liberally from this document (My translation of the 1904 French version). Nguyễn Tấn's comments on Bùi Tá Hán and on the structure he allegedly created are as follows:

---

[23] "Trấn Man" can be interpreted as "protect against barbarians," and "Sơn Phòng" as "protect against the mountains."

Our province was originally part of the kingdom of Champa and constituted the region of Cổ Lũy Động. It was annexed by Annam by the Hồ kings while the legitimate Trần dynasty was in its last stages of decadence, but soon it became a part of Champa again. Meanwhile king Lê Hồng Đức conquered it around 1471 and populated it with North Vietnamese colonists, because it had large sparsely populated areas.

The first governor of the area was the Duke of the Province (Trấn Quận Công)[24] who had the title of Commander of Northern Armies (Bắc Quan Đố Đốc) and was sent during the reign of Lê Chánh Hoà. After the annexation the Annamite domination was achieved progressively.[25]

Here Nguyễn Tấn lists, in the order of their annexation, the five highland districts of the province over which the Vietnamese court gained control. They were La Thu Dao, Nuoc Ly, Thanh Cu Nguyên, Phu An Nguyên, and Ba To Nguyen.[26]

According to tradition, an indigenous chief, called a Giáo Dịch, was at the head of the administration of the district. Those of the three nguyên[23] were organized administratively. At this time the aboriginal population was small in number and in density. The savages, pressed by misery, made themselves the servants of our compatriots.

Then, during the reign of Lê Chánh Trị, this whole region was placed under the authority of the Nguyễn lord, or Thái Tổ Gia Dự Hoàng Đế, which resulted, during the next six or seven successors of this king, in an era of peace which was not troubled by a single attempt at independence. Lowland and highland people lived side by side in complete security. (Nguyễn Tấn, 1904:462-463).

Later, Nguyễn Tấn repeats: "Under the reign of Lê Chánh Hoà, the General of the Northern Armies (Bắc Quan Đố Đốc), Duke of the Province (Trấn Quận Công) was named the governor of our area. One can still observe on the frontier some vestiges of posts created by this governor to guard himself against the highland people." (Nguyễn Tấn, 1904:789). In a final

---

[24] This is Bùi Tá Hán, who will be discussed presently.

[25] Lê Chánh Hòa refers to the second reign period of Lê Hi Tồng (1676-1705). This must be an error. Probably Nguyễn Hòa (Lê Trang Tông, 1533-1548) is the reign period intended.

[26] "Nguyên" or "Nguôn" apparently were subdistricts in the highland area.

section he reviews the accomplishments of each mandarin who gained fame in dealing with the highland people of Quảng Nam. In this section he describes Bùi Tá Hán as follows:

Bùi Tá Hán, native of North Vietnam.

Under the reign of Lê Chánh Hoà he was Duke of the province, General of the Armies of North Vietnam. In this role he was sent to be governor of Quảng Nam.

The highland people obeyed him completely, as if they were his servants. Both highland and lowland people lived together peaceably.

It is said that the highland people were treated as his servants or slaves. There is no proof for this allegation.

At his death in 1568 he received the posthumous title of Thái Bảo. A temple was built for his cult.

One can still observe, in the high country of the frontiers, some of the ruins of forts which are alleged to have been built by him, as well as some of his orchards. Whether they were, in fact, those which he left is impossible to ascertain. The highland people always invoke his name in their prayers. This proves that he was a virtuous man. (Nguyễn Tấn, 1904:794).

In another context Nguyễn Tấn states:

Originally, the government divided the area into four subdistricts (nguyên), subjected to tribute. These four districts were Do Bong and Cu Ba in the district of Binh Son, Phu Ba in the district of Chuong Nghia, and Ba To in the District of Mo Duc. The following functionaries were created:

Two Cai Quan and two Con Quan in the district of Da Bong and a Cai Quan and a Con Quan in each of the districts of Cu Ba, Phu Ba, and Ba To.

The district of Da Bong had more frequent and more developed commercial relationships with the lowland people than the other three districts.

These functionaries had the responsibility of seeing that the commercial agents (Thương Hồ) paid the taxes which amounted to 1,450 ligatures per year, plus the sum of twenty ligatures as an advance payment on the cinnamon tribute (Nguyễn Tấn, 1904:706-707).

In these sections Nguyễn Tấn telescopes long periods of history into several paragraphs. Consequently, one can only speculate as to which of the details of the administration can actually be attributed to Bùi Tá Hán and which followed much later, perhaps under Gia Long. Particularly in the last excerpt, he does not indicate whether "originally" actually refers to the administration of Bùi Tá Hán or to later periods. Since the names of the districts differ from those cited earlier (page 25), it seems reasonable to conclude that he is referring to a later period. Nor does it seem reasonable to suppose that he would have known the amount of tribute charged in the middle of the 16th century. The figures for tribute must refer to a much later period.

Nevertheless, Nguyễn Tấn clearly felt that the contact between Bùi Tá Hán and the highland people was significant and profound and that it established something of a pattern to be emulated later on. The details of this pattern will be taken up later. Some of its major elements are mentioned in these sections by Nguyễn Tấn. They are:

1. The imposition of taxes or tribute.

2. The establishment of patented commercial agents or agencies (Giáo Dịch, Thương Hồ who were held responsible for collecting taxes.

3. A military structure with frontier posts or forts to keep the peace, and particularly, control the highland people. Military settlements or colonies (Đôn Điền) are specifically mentioned, ". . . with the double role of police and agriculture." (PMTL, 716)

4. An administrative structure divided into hamlets, districts, etc., with highland authorities at the very lowest levels.

Bùi Tá Hán's administration was allegedly followed by 200 years of peace and tranquility, during which the highland and lowland people of Quảng Nam allegedly lived side by side without incident (Nguyễn Tấn, 1904: 462-463). Whatever the facts of the case I have not been able to find historical material on lowland-highland relationships during this period. In the middle of the 18th century a considerable amount of attention again goes to the highland people, not only in Quảng Nam; but also further south in Phú Yên. During the reign of Nguyễn Phúc Khóat (1738-1765), Nguyễn Cư Trình was assigned to pacify the highland people of Quảng Nam

(DNTL, Vol. 1:211-213). In 1751 the Jarai kings paid tribute to the lowland court (DNTL, Vol. 1:212), this being the first tribute mission from these kings which I have been able to confirm in court records, but that is the topic of the next section of this paper.

Thus, one is led to conclude that, although it seems reasonable to infer that direct administrative relationships between the Vietnamese court and highland people began sometime during the 16th century, the precise dates for specific aspects of this development cannot, as yet, be identified.

I shall now turn to a consideration of the other pattern of relationship which is prominent in Vietnamese history. This is tributary relationships with more remote highland people who are regarded by the court as semi-independent political entities.

Tributary Relationships with Remote Highland People

One of the more interesting aspects of relationships between the lowland court and the highland people of Central and South Vietnam concerns the two Jarai "kings" or sorcerers, referred to as the King of Fire and the King of Water. Their titles in Jarai are, respectively, Patao Pui and Patao Ea. In Vietnamese they are usually referred to as Thủy Xá and Hoả Xá, referring, simultaneously, to a role such as king and a territorial jurisdiction. The French referred to them as "Sadets". They are, and the King of Fire still exists today, essentially sorcerers who were and are known throughout the Central Highlands, including areas inhabited by other tribes such as the Rhade. Because they were well known, and, no doubt, because they maintained contacts with both the Vietnamese court and the court at Angkor, they had at least potential political significance in the Central Highlands.[27]

These kings represent a style of lowland-highland relationship quite different from that which developed in Quảng Nam, Quảng Ngãi, and Bình Định. They were treated as tributary states, a status which was apparently regarded by the lowland court as a benevolence which it

---

[27] For more detailed discussions of the King of Fire and King of Water see Ezzaui (1940), Jouin (1951), Nghiêm Thẩm (1962), and Bourotte (1955:31-33).

bestowed upon the highland people. They were assigned a regular schedule for submitting tribute to the court. Thus, formally, their status vis-a-vis the court at Huế was similar to that of the kingdoms of Luang Prabang, Vientaine, and Cambodia.

There is some fascinating information regarding this relationship in Nguyễn dynasty documents arising from the fact that the Jarai simultaneously carried on "diplomatic" relationships with the Cambodian court and with Huế, a discovery which troubled the court of Huế when it occurred. However, this is not the place to present these details (Nghiêm Thẩm, 1962:136-144). The issue here is the antiquity of these relationships with the Vietnamese court.

Henri Maitre stated:

> It is probable, therefore, that the Annamite armies established only a few settlers among the Jarai; one thing is certain, and that is that in 1558 the Jarai kings, probably as the result of a defeat, recognized the supremacy of Annam and became vassals of Huế. The Annals of the Ministry of Rites state, in effect, that from that year the Thủy Xá and Hoả Xá regularly paid tribute every three years. The tribute was sent through the province of Phú Yên and was made up of elephant tusks and rhinoceros horns. During the centuries, this act of vassalage toward Huế was observed faithfully, it did not stop until 1841 (Maitre, 1912:448-449) (My translation).

This 1558 date has been repeated frequently with Maitre as the authority. (Bourotte, 1955:23; Nghiêm Thẩm, 1962:133; Nyo, 1937:50; Bùi Đình, 1963:87). It turns out that Maitre did not consult the "Annals" himself. He refers in a footnote to statements made by a certain Captain Luce who prepared a report on the alleged hegemony of Vietnam over the area to the east bank of the Mekong. It is from Luce that he received his information although he suggests, in the footnote, that Luce obtained his information from either Khâm Định Đại Nam Hội Điển Sự Lệ or the Đại Nam Liệt Truyện Tiên Biên (Maitre, 1912:449). The relevant portion of the former is now available in the National Script (Quốc Ngữ) and in it the dates of tribute missions from the Jarai go back no farther than 1829 (Nhu' Viễn, 1966:67; 107-108). I have not seen the complete text of the Liệt Truyện. However, Nghiêm Thẩm has translated selections dealing with the highland people in an article on the highland people (Nghiêm Thẩm, 1962:130-150). The first few lines of his translation from the Liệt Truyện bear quoting here:

The two countries of Thủy Xá and Hoả Xá, are in the land of Nam Bàn. When king Lê Thánh Tôn succeeded in defeating Champa, he established the noble descendents of that country (in the land of Nam Bàn). He established the mountain of Thách Bi, with 50 villages on the West, as the boundary. In that country there is the mountain of Bà Nam which is very high. The king of Thủy Xá is on the East and the king of Hoả Xá is on the West of that mountain.

The Nguyễn court, at the beginning, realized that the countries of Thủy Xá and Hoả Xá bordered on the province of Phu Yên. Every five years they sent someone to bring gifts to the two kings of that country.

During the reign of king Thế Tôn (Nguyễn Phúc Khoát , 1738-1765), the thirteenth year, the king of the two countries of Thủy Xá and Hoả Xá sent an emissary with tribute (Nghiêm Thẩm, 1962:136-137). (My translation)

There is no other mention of the earlier periods in the portions of the Liệt Truyện translated by Nghiêm Thẩm. Thus, although tributary relationships are said to have existed since the beginning of the Nguyễn family in the South (1558), there is no evidence, in these materials, of specific tributary missions until around 1751, nearly 200 years later.[28] These are, of course, exactly the same years which were said to have been peaceful in the special highland administrative unit in Quảng Nam. No doubt the tributary relationships with the Jarai did begin before 1751. Whether they began as early as 1558 we do not know. It seems reasonable to suggest that the confidence of Maitre and his captain Luce in the earlier date had as much to do with their desire to prove historical hegemony of Vietnam over the highland areas as it did with specific evidence they found in the "Annals."

Conclusions

Several points emerge from this discussion. First, in spite of the ambiguity regarding actual dates, it is clear that these contacts existed very early. By the middle of the 18th century Quảng Nam, Quảng Ngãi, and Bình Định, as well as Phu Yên, Khánh Hoà, Bình Thuận, and Gia Định provinces had elements of an administration devised specifically for the highland people

---

[28] The DNTL, though not one of the sources mentioned by Maitre, also states that there was a tributary mission from the Jarai kings in 1751 (DNTL, Vol. 1:214).

who were immediately accessible and tributary relationships had been established and were being observed more or less regularly with the kings of the Jarai. It seems reasonable to conclude that in the North (the Sơn Phòng) these relationships developed during the middle of the l6th century.[29]

Secondly, a much more thorough study of documents must be undertaken to fill in the hiatus from approximately 1560 to 1750. The materials available to me are almost entirely those of the Nguyễn dynasty, which were not written until well into the 19th century when this dynasty had reached its apogee. Other sources should be examined for information during this era.

---

[29] Charles Joiner has written: "Despite the historic march to the South of the Vietnamese after the end of the 1,000-year era of Chinese suzerainty, and the victories of the Vietnamese over both the Chams and the various tribal groups during this southward migration, the imperial regime at Huế never succeeded in permanently penetrating the highlands, where the tribesmen went to seek refuge and to maintain their communal identity. As Joseph Buttinger has noted, the last emperor of Vietnam, Tự Đức, did make a futile attempt to extend Vietnamese governmental authority into the highlands after 1863, but this effort failed entirely of enduring success" (Joiner, 1961:21). While the literal truth of this claim depends entirely upon what is meant by ". . . never succeeded in permanently penetrating the highlands. . ," the statement is somewhat misleading. There was substantial penetration and direct administration of highland areas in Quảng Nam. This penetration was simultaneously carefully established for international political purposes, and vigorously condemned internally by early French writers, nearly all of whom were military officers or colonial administrators, which hardly made them objective observers. It is further misleading in that the area regarded as highlands tends to depend upon its political status vis-a-vis the Huế court. Thus, whenever land was penetrated and claimed by lowland colonists, it was no longer regarded as being in the highlands. Furthermore, it completely disregards the long standing inter-dependence of highland people and the lowland court for trade. Finally, Tự Đức's attempt in 1863 apparently refers to the campaign of Nguyễn Tấn, which was: (1) not an attempt to penetrate the highlands generally, being directed only at pacification of the Sơn Phòng area, and (2) was not futile by Nguyễn Tấn's account (See also Durand's reports on the same area, 1900). Indeed, the French had to dismantle the Sơn Phòng administration in 1899, so it can hardly have been a complete failure.

PATTERNS AND OBJECTIVES OF RELATIONSHIPS BETWEEN LOWLAND AND HIGHLAND PEOPLE

Administration of Accessible Highland

A distinction has already been made between accessible highland people and those who were not accessible. These are, of course, merely extremes on a continuum with some groups falling well between them. Among those groups which were accessible and, consequently, subject to direct administration, different details emerged in different areas. Henri Maitre regarded the structure of the Sơn Phòng as the basic pattern which was copied everywhere in the South where contacts with highland people were substantial. In order to consider this question it is necessary to review the history of this special administrative unit.

I have already discussed the origin of this "barbarian province." In 1751 Nguyễn Cư Trinh was assigned to pacify the highland people of the region again. Few details are available on his accomplishments. However, it is interesting that he recommended that administrative functions such as taxation be removed from local officials and turned over to provincial officials because the local officials were corrupt and incited the people to rebel (DNTL, Vol. 1:211-213).

In 1804 Gia Long reorganized the barbarian province, christening it the Trấn Man, and granted it to Nguyễn Công Toản as a hereditary fiefdom because Công Toản had performed heroic exploits in pacifying highland people in 1773 while fighting against the Tây Sơn (Bùi Đình, 1960:87; PMTL, 714, 790, 795). In 1819 Lê Van Duyệt was called to pacify the highland people of the area again and he, in desperation, built a wall 90 kilometers long with 115 military posts in order to contain the belligerent highland people of the area. Apparently ruins of his wall were still visible in the early 1960's (Bùi Đình, 1963: 88).

In the early 1860's the highland people of the area again became quiescent, perhaps because of a reduction in the military strength of the local troops due to demands made elsewhere to resist the French. Large numbers of lowland villages in the area had been abandoned because they had been over run by the highland people. Nguyễn Tấn, a native of the area and a descendent of Nguyễn Công Toản, was the provincial judge (Ấn Sát) of Thái Nguyên. He became concerned about his home province and requested that the court assign him to pacify the barbarian province. He was reassigned in 1863, and between 1863 and 1869 he pacified the highland people and reorganized the administration and police of the area. It was then christened the Sơn Phòng (Durand, 1900:288; PMTL, Bùi Đình, 1963:89). The administration he established is described in detail in the PMTL. Nguyễn Tấn was given the title of Sub-Province Commissioner (Tiểu Phủ Sứ). His administration was essentially military (Maitre, 1912:510; Durand, 1900: 285). There was a complicated system of 100 frontier posts, along Lê Văn Duyệt's wall. Highland people held offices as high as the sub-district (Nguyên, Nguôn) level. Apparently the elaborate system of commercial agents to whom taxes were normally "farmed out" was suppressed in favor of direct administration of these functions (PMTL, 709; Bùi Đình, 1963:89-91; Durand, 1900, 288-289). According to Durand, it was much later, under Nguyễn Khánh, that civilian administration was again instituted (Durand, 1900:289). Durand also said that the Sơn Phòng remained in the hands of Nguyễn Tấn's descendents until it was finally abolished by the French in 1899 (Durand, 1900:285).

Maitre regarded this as the paradigm for the administration of highland people further south. However, the Sơn Phòng was almost exclusively concerned with local military matters, that is, the pacification of the highland people, no doubt because of the bellicosity of the highland people of this area. Maitre himself recognized that the "normal" concerns of the court in the highlands were primarily fiscal (Maitre, 1912:470). The frequent attacks upon lowland villages in this particular area resulted, no doubt, from a combination of factors. The highland people of the area may have been involved in the slave trade in Laos; it was not unusual for lowlanders to appear as slaves in these markets. They had, apparently, been seized in Central Vietnam. Furthermore, lowlanders had penetrated unusually far into the highlands in this area because of the topography, creating severe competition for land. Further south, the lowland administration of highland areas was much more concerned with fiscal matters, and there was less involvement in direct administration for the purposes of pacification. Nor was there the long history of repeated revolts. The characteristic feature of these other areas was the commercial agents who, for the exclusive privilege of trading with the highland people, were required to collect the taxes assessed from them.

It is difficult, therefore, to generalize about the pattern of administration. If anything stands out it is the pragmatic approach of provincial officials and of the Huế court in dealing with the highland people. There were a number of mechanisms used, depending upon the circumstances. They included the establishment of a "barbarian" provincial administration if necessary, the establishment of military and civilian colonies (Đôn Điền and Dinh Điền) by both provincial administrations and the central administration, the enfranchisement of commercial agents with exclusive rights to trade in highland areas, and taxation. Bourotte's conclusion seems correct; that the objectives of the administration of the highland people were threefold:

1. To maintain peace, in particular, to keep the highland people from raiding lowland villages.

2. To collect taxes from the highland people.

3. To reserve trade and commerce with the highland people for the court (Bourotte, 1955:27).

I would only add that the court wished to retain the prerogative to open frontier lands, since areas occupied by highland people were usually seen to be sparsely populated (PMTL, 462) and fertile. Furthermore, it should be emphasized that, at this time, the products provided by the highland people were very important to the court (Durand, 1900:308-309).

The most important theme running through the relationships with accessible people as long as they remained pacified was fiscal. The Sơn Phòng was, from this point of view, an exception, and it was so because of the bellicosity of the highland people of the area. When pacification was achieved, attention was normally directed at taxation and trade. Even the bizarre (to lowland people) customs of the people of the highlands were accepted and the abuses of local officials were overlooked as long as no one rebelled, trade was not disrupted, and the taxes were paid.

Relationships with Tributary Barbarians

If those stated above were the objectives of the administration of the more accessible people of the highlands, what were the objectives of the tributary relationships with those who were more distant? Because they were considered to be tributary or vassal states, they were placed in a category with Luang Prabang, Vientiane, Burma, France, England, Trấn Ninh (in Laos), and, on occasion, also the highland minority groups of North Vietnam such as the Thổ, Nùng, Mán, and Meò, a very diverse group indeed (Woodside, 1971: 237, 244).

To answer this question it is useful to establish that these relationships were, indeed, important to the lowland court. On this point, it is interesting to note that the Huế court apparently took the initiative in contacts with the Jarai. The Liệt Truyện states: "Every five years they (The Vietnamese kings) sent someone to bring gifts to the two kings of that country. . ." (Nghiêm Thẩm, 1962:137) The Đại Nam Thực Lục states:

> When the country was young (when Đại Nam was young), because they
> (the Jarai kings) shared a border with Phú Yên, every five years a person was sent
> to those countries (of the Jarai kings) with gifts (brocade garments, hats, brass
> pots, iron pans, and porcelain ware). Immediately upon receiving the gifts, the
> kings of those two countries prepared local products[30] (aloe wood, beeswax, deer
> antlers, bile of bear, and male elephants) to give in return. They then sent an
> emissary to pay tribute. The king then rewarded them and allowed them to return
> (DNTL, Vol. 1:214).

The fact that the Huế court took the initiative indicates that it considered the relationship important. When it was discovered that the Jarai kings maintained tributary relationships with the court at Angkor, an immediate investigation was ordered. The story of this event is very interesting, but it cannot be recounted in detail here. Very briefly, during the time that Trương Minh Giảng was serving as the "protector" of Cambodia, apparently one of the two Jarai kings appeared in person in Cambodia requesting an audience with the king of Cambodia. This was

---

[30] The "Lịch Triều" actually lists two aromatic woods, "kỳ nam" and "trầm hương." According to Maitre (1909:155-156) "kỳ nam " is the heartwood of the aloe and " trầm hương" is the sapwood. The former is more desirable.

reported to Huế and Minh Mạng immediately ordered an investigation. The investigation was not carried out at the time because the Cambodians successfully rebelled against the Vietnamese administration. However, later in the year an investigation was carried out under the supervision of the provincial officials in Phú Yên. This mission is discussed in detail by Nghiêm Thẩm (Nghiêm Thẩm, 1962:136-144).

What, then, were the objectives of this relationship from the point of view of the Huế court? The charge given by Minh Mạng regarding the investigation of the Thủy Xá and Hoả Xá (in 1840) was as follows:

> . . . if the tribal chief (Thủy Xá) is still in the area of Sơn Bốc (Cambodia), you must receive him warmly immediately and ask him what is the origin of his tribal group. Ask him how long they have been there, what are the borders of their area, which mountains and rivers, cities, they have, and what the rulers and people are like. You must also ask them whether their area is worthy of being called a country or not, or whether they, in fact, live in caves like the Lao tribes. You must ask them what the customs of their people are and whether they know how to distinguish between the rank of a king and his subjects (ie. know social distinctions, are civilized). . . you must also ask them what kind of magic the tribal chief has (Nghiêm Thẩm 1962:139).

The concern with borders and with the level of political sophistication seems to indicate an interest in the strategic importance of the hill tribes. When Thiệu Triệu became king, he sent a letter to the Thủy Xá announcing his ascendancy to the throne, praising the Thủy Xá for his fidelity, and, charging him to: ". . . worship the large country (Vietnam) and fear Heaven; you must be careful not to oppose the way of Heaven. Be friendly with all neighboring countries and watch the borders, in order that you may be able to benefit from the widespread and profound magnanimity (of the king)" (Nghiêm Thẩm. 1962:146). Again, the concern with maintaining peace on the frontiers is evident. No doubt an additional concern was trade, but it seems unlikely that the tribute paid every three years was great enough in volume to be very important to the court. No doubt the taxes imposed upon accessible highland people and the system of commercial agents, who occasionally penetrated very far into the hinterland, supplied a much larger volume of these desired commodities.

The populations on the frontiers have been a problem to the Vietnamese state throughout its existence (Hoàng Xuân Hãn, 1966: 101, 110-111); McAlister, 1967:786-797). In the North it was always possible for the Chinese to stir up trouble by using them. Similarly, in the South both internal and external enemies could use them and their areas as a base from which to attack the lowland villages and fortresses. The problem still exists today. Consequently, the court had a strong interest in maintaining order on the frontiers. Following the rule of "using barbarians to fight barbarians" (dùng rợ chống với rợ) attributed to Nguyễn Cư Trinh (Lê Ngọc Trụ and Phạm Văn Luật, 1951:49), the court's concern about the frontiers was greatly facilitated by having some extra-village political entity on the frontier with which it could deal. It may have been more the result of geography than the political influence of the Thủy Xá and Hoả Xá that their "country" had never rebelled. After all, the Jarai and Rhade of the high plateau had few convenient routes to the coast, and consequently their lands had not been occupied by lowland settlers and they had not been molested by the ubiquitous "commercial agents". They were simply not as accessible.

Lê Văn Quyền, the scout sent into the highland areas from the provincial offices at Phú Yên in 1840, reported that: ". . . the local chiefs, they have the power of life and death over the people, and are frequently at war. The chief of state (Thủy Xá or Hoả Xá), does not involve himself in these affairs" (Nghiêm Thẩm, 1962: 142). When the French arrived, several influential chiefs were able to terrorize whole regions, without any intervention by the Thủy Xá or Hoả Xá.[31] Thus, it is clear that the explicit political power of these kings was slight, and the court seems to have sensed this and been somewhat anxious about it. Nevertheless, it was very convenient to deal with this area through them and, since they had never rebelled and since the tribute was usually sent regularly, the court was satisfied that, at least with respect to the Thủy Xá and Hoả Xá, the empirical world had been made to correspond with its hierarchical model.

---

[31] See Condominas' introduction to Kdam Yi on the role of these "local chiefs" (Condominas, 1953).

Woodside has suggested that the objective of the tributary relationship with the Jarai kings was to inflate the status of the Vietnamese emperor (Woodside, 1971:238). He points out that, on the one hand, this required that the political importance of the Jarai kings be inflated, whereas, on the other hand, the relationship of Vietnam to genuine political entities such as Burma had to be seriously misrepresented.

It seems to me that, if the form of the relationship is considered rather than the absolute status of the respective political entities, applying the Chinese model to the Jarai, the Lao, and the Northern minorities was quite congruent with empirical reality. Proportionally the model was appropriate. No doubt the emperor was humbled by the realization that those whom he could call his vassals included kings with tenuous authority over "50 villages" and Lao tribes "who lived in caves." However, if he could accept this, the model was surprisingly accurate, not least in that the relationship, itself, tended to enhance the supra-village political entity with which the court was dealing and thereby made the frontiers more manageable. It was, as Woodside recognized, a very useful model in the Southeast Asian environment (Woodside, 1971:238)

The model was vulnerable on two counts. First, those whose status was such that they could be called the Vietnamese emperor's vassals did not really have enduring political power. They were ephemeral "kinglets." Second, the concept was static, and was not designed to describe an expanding state. When territory previously occupied by a tributary tribal group became attractive and accessible to lowland settlers, ambiguous relationships emerged, with the same tribal groups simultaneously being administered directly by the bureaucracy and bringing tribute (Woodside, 1971:244).

One can suggest the sequence of events which may have occurred under these circumstances. First, by virtue of being accessible and attractive to lowland settlers, contacts between lowlanders and highlanders would increase. These contacts would result in unrest and, quite possibly, attacks upon lowland villagers by highlanders, partly because their land was being taken but partly also because of the agitation of lowland dissidents who were frequently found on the frontier. For example, Dr. Yersin encountered a band of 80 bandits in the highlands who planned to attack the provincial headquarters at Phan Rang (Yersin, 1935:184). These attacks would require "pacification" and the establishment of military forts, with the eventual establishment of direct administration of the highland people if necessary, or the establishment of a system of intermediaries if that proved adequate. These events would have eroded the influence of the sorcerer kings, or perhaps it would be more correct to say that their lack of political power would be exposed in that they would not be able, even if they wanted to, to prevent local chieftains from attacking lowland villages. Tributary missions would cease or at least become irregular.

Thus it seems that, whereas the objectives of the administration of accessible highland people were primarily fiscal, the objectives of the tributary relationships with remote highland people were primarily to make the frontiers explicable and manageable, that is, political.

The Products Exchanged

Trade and taxes were the principal mechanisms through which products were exchanged between lowland people and the accessible highland people. Some highland people, no doubt, contributed simultaneously through trade and taxes, as well as tribute. For example, Dr. Yersin visited a Rhade village in the Mdrack area which paid tribute to the Thủy Xá and Hoả Xá, tribute which, no doubt, contributed to that paid by the latter to the Huế court. At the same time, enfranchised "tax farmers" or "commercial agents" existed in this area, and trade was carried on directly with the mandarins in Khánh Hòa at the market place in Ninh Hòa by elephant caravan (Aymonier, 1886:217-228). However, tribute did not involve the extent of contact, or the gross amount of product, as did trade and taxation, so it has been discussed separately.

Trade was ubiquitous, variously regulated during different periods of time and, I believe, of great importance to both highland people and to the lowland economy generally and to the Huế court in particular. The highland people depended upon this trade, among other things, for salt (Aymonier, 1895:325; Maitre, 1912:498-499, 500), dried fish (PMTL, 468), ceremonial gongs and jars (Maitre, 1912:498-499), English cottons (Maitre, 1912:498-499), and lowland clothing, especially Chinese garments with which they allegedly preferred to appear before lowland merchants (PMTL, 468). The lowland people, and especially the court, obtained from this trade hardwoods (DNTL, Vol. 26:146-147; Maitre, 1912:503-504; Aymonier, 1886:292-296), aromatic woods such as aloe wood and eagle wood (Aymonier, 1886:8), cinnamon (Maitre, 1912:513-514,516), beeswax (DNTL, Vol. 2:193), ivory (Maitre, 1912:498-499), rhinoceros horns (Neiss, 1880:3), elephants (DNTL, Vol. 1:212-213; Maitre, 1912:498-499), horses (Maitre, 1912:498-499), and many other items specific to the different areas. An example of these locally specific trade products was a highland village which was found to be selling dugout canoes to the lowland people in the Donnai valley (Gautier, 1935:46). The attraction of these highland products to the lowland court may be inferred from a statement by Phan Huy Chú regarding the district of Hoài Nhân, which encompasses the "more than fifty villages" subject to the Jarai kings:

> This one district has its full share of material possessions, together with the districts of Tư Nghiã and Thang Hòa, it can be categorized as wealthy. There are many natural resources: aloe wood, rhinoceros horns, gold, silver, sea turtles, precious stones, beeswax, sugar, honey, oil, lacquer, green areca nuts, black pepper, fish, salt, and all kinds of high quality lumber, and rice in abundance. Horses are born in the mountains, and they can be found in herds of up to one hundred thousand. The local people used to ride to the market on horses (Phan Huy Chú. 1960 (Vol. 1): 138) .

Maitre quotes an Italian missionary, who said that the highland people, referred to as the kẻ mọi (savages) by him, provided the precious eagle wood and aloe wood ". . . which is the most precious merchandise which can be found in Cochinchina for export to foreign countries" (Maitre, 1912:458). Thus, this trade may have played a special role in Vietnamese foreign trade. Durand provides a detailed list of trade items with their prices, including both imports and exports, from the Sơn Phòng area of Quảng Ngãi. All of it, according to him, was less important than the slave trade. This area, of course, involved the bellicose highlanders who were known to be involved in the slave trade which flourished in Laos and Cambodia at the time (Durand. 1900:308-310). Among the imports to this area were hatchets, knives, lances, various brass pots and bowls, brass bracelets, silver earrings, precious stones, gongs, cymbals, ceremonial jars, and cottons. Among the exports were tobacco, betel, beeswax, rattan, cotton, areca nuts, cardamon, deer antlers, rice, cinnamon, several varieties of aloe wood, elephant tusks, and rhinoceros horns.

This trade expressed a degree of interdependence which has been inadequately recognized. Salt was probably the crucial item from the point of view of the highland people, since they depended upon this lowland trade for it. In a revealing comment, Yersin reports to have encountered a Mnong village which had never seen a lowlander and where the people did not use salt (1935:196). Unfortunately, it is impossible to make an estimate of the total volume of trade in any one product. Maitre calculated that Darlac province had sold 161 elephants during the years of 1899 to 1908, and these included only those from villages which were considered to be "pacified" (Maitre, 1909:150).

Taxes were levied by the lowland court upon the accessible or directly administered highland people, usually both in cash and in kind. These taxes were significant, and frequently quite onerous. The court recognized that taxes were frequently a cause of highland uprisings, and frequently reduced or suspended them when such uprisings occurred (Nyo, 1937:55; DNTL, Vol. 1:212; DNTL, Vol. 3:103; PMTL, 709). Some villages near Cochinchina sought to be annexed to the new French colony in order to escape the taxes they had to pay through the mandarins at Phan Thiết, perhaps the first example of how the very presence of a third power drove a wedge between highland and lowland societies (Yersin, 1935:169). Some rather detailed information is available on the amounts of taxes levied upon the highland people in Khanh Hoa province when the French first arrived (Maitre, 1912:496-498).

Another method of obtaining highland products was to requisition them. It was common for the court to requisition the service of lowland artisans. From the highland people lumber, as well as labor, was sometimes requisitioned in a similar fashion. Hòa cơ referred to requisitions for public works and Hòa mãi referred to requisitions for the royal family (Maitre, 1912:503-504). In these requisitions the provincial officials were charged with obtaining the materials at a fixed price. In the case of materials destined for the royal family, three-fifths of the price was to be paid in advance, the remainder being paid when the order was delivered. Because local officials had the responsibility of dealing with the highland people, this system was subject to abuse. It was reported that in Bình Thuận province that highland people seldom, if ever, actually received the payment due them for requisitioned products (Maitre, 1912:503; Aymonier, 1885:292-296).

The DNTL records an interesting incident involving the purchase of wood from the highland people on order from the court. The highland people had attacked the lowlanders and burned a supply of wood which the highland people had provided, but for which they had not yet been paid. The responsible official reported that they had "volunteered" to delay receipt of payment until all of the wood was delivered, and that he had not yet had the time to make the calculations required and to pay them. The official was severely reprimanded and punished by the court, and it was pointed out that payments should have been made in advance from the local treasury. "How could one expect to obtain wood without paying for it?" the Court inquired (DNTL, Vol. 16:146-147).

Intermediaries or Commercial Agents

Probably the most characteristic feature of relationships between lowland and highland societies was the existence of a group of people who served as intermediaries, commercial agents, or, perhaps more accurately, as tax farmers. They were enfranchised to engage in trade among the highland people, in exchange for which they were held responsible for collecting the tax assessments and delivering these to the provincial officials to be forwarded to the court. Apparently these franchises were purchased, at least in some areas. Aymonier reported that one agent had paid 700 ligatures and another had paid 800 ligatures for the right to exploit the highland people for a year (Aymonier, 1885:325). In these cases the agents simply taxed the highland people's trade at a rate of 4%. A footnote to the PMTL, apparently written by the anonymous French translator, implies that the Sơn Phòng also had highland people especially enfranchised to carry on trade in lowland areas (PMTL, 707). Bourotte claims that this institution, under the rubric of the term "giao dịch" (commercial agent)[32] was instituted during the

---

[32] A footnote in the French version of the PMTL states, of giáo dịch: "par le mot de relation giáo dịch significait litteralement: echange commercial, il faut comprendre le trafic ou l'echange

42

16th century although he presents no evidence for such an early date besides the very ambiguous statement of the PMTL. These commercial agents were referred to differently at different times and in different areas. One frequently used term was Thuộc Lại which simply means low level functionary (Maitre) 1912:499-500). Ten other terms which appear are Các Lái, Lái Buôn, Giao Dịch, Dịch Mục, Thừa Biên, Thử Ngữ, Thương Hồ, Thông Dịch (Tông Dịch), Lãnh Mãi, Đo Đưa (Aymonier) 1886:27). These terms connote either a commercial relationship or an interpreter. Apparently in some areas at least they were seen to be interpreters, having language skills. Apparently these agents were lowland Vietnamese[33] (Durand, 1900: 299; Maitre, 1912:500; PMTL, 709) although the PMTL seems to imply that a Giao Dịch, who was an indigenous chief, served this function in the Sơn Phòng (PMTL, 462). It seems clear that they were lowlanders after 1802, when more information becomes available. It is also possible that this group is, in fact, quite heterogeneous, and that there were different functions for people bearing the different titles. There is very little information available on their specific functions.

Although these people were commercial agents, presumably restricted to trading and thereby collecting taxes, their actual functions sometimes exceeded that. Thus, for example, it was reported that the intermediaries in Bình Thuận had certain direct administrative responsibilities vis-a-vis the highland people (Maitre) 1912:501; Aymonier) 1885:318).

These agents frequently operated with a large entourage of assistants, subcontractors, and collaborators. In the Sơn Phòng, for example, they subcontracted their trading rights to the district and village chiefs established by the Sơn Phòng administration (Durand) 1900:299). Everywhere they were said to have been assisted and sometimes controlled by Chinese merchants who apparently supplied them with trade goods on credit (Maitre, 1912:498,500, 515). These Chinese merchants illegally exported many of the forest products thus obtained to China (Maitre, 1912:500: Aymonier, 1885:319). In Quẳng Nam these agents, enfranchised by the Minh

---

commercial auquel se livraient des Annamites qu'avaient des lettres patentes a cet effet et qui n'etaient autres que ces agents commerciaux ayant la ferme des impots" (PMTL, 709).

[33] It was said that Nguyễn Nhạc of the Tây Sơn had originally been a tax collector among the highland people of the An Khê area (Bourotte, 1955:31).

Mạng administration to have exclusive rights to the cinnamon trade for the benefit of Prince Kiên An, eventually subcontracted these rights to local agents who lived near the highland people and spoke their languages, resulting in a complicated hierarchically organized business enterprise (Maitre, 1912:515). This enterprise was welded together by credit relationships, no doubt ultimately controlled by Chinese merchants.

The commercial agents did not restrict themselves to trading with the accessible or pacified highland people. They frequently ranged far and wide in the highlands, far behind the frontier (Verneville, 1882: 296). Maitre reports that they reached the Mdrac plateau from the Sông Ba valley (from Qui Nhơn) and from Ninh Hòa (Maitre, 1912:499, 506-507). Dr. Yersin encountered several of them operating in the Koho Maa area during an expedition in 1893. By this time the French had already begun to eliminate them so Dr. Yersin arrested those he encountered and delivered them to the French authorities in Phan Thiết (Yersin, 1935:175-176). The same year he also encountered an agent living with his wife and "personnel" in a Rhade village in the Mdrac area. Gautier encountered lowlanders among highland people along the Đồng Nai river in 1882 (Gautier, 1935:46). They were there to farm as well as to engage in trade. Whereas these agents frequently exploited those highland people who were near the coast, especially in Binh Thuận (Aymonier, 1885: 324-329), they were largely at the mercy of the highland people when they penetrated far into the highlands (Yersin, 1935:193). In fact, the chiefs of Mdrac and of the Darlac plateau used their liaison with these lowland agents to strengthen themselves vis-a-vis their competitors (Maitre, 1909:57).

These agents operated in several different ways. In the Sơn Phòng area, in Binh Thuận, and in Khánh Hòa, annual trade fairs, called Trương Sấp or Trương Thị, were organized by the commercial agents (Maitre, 1912:511; Aymonier, 1885:323-324; Aymonier, 1886:27-28). At these fairs the highland people brought their goods, which were carefully measured and given to the provincial mandarins. Then they were "rewarded" with goods presented to them by the agents. The Ninh Hòa fair must have been quite picturesque, as it was described by Aymonier:

The tribute paying people to the north bring their tax once a year to Ninh Hòa and a high mandarin from the citadel goes out to receive it, together with numerous presents for himself and his entourage. These presents double or triple the actual tax. The savages frequently come great distances, riding on elephants, in groups of 40 or 50. The mandarins buy elephants from them for the king's service. And, on the occasion of this annual tribute collection, a kind of grand fair takes place at Trương Sấp, which is one league from the market place, in the Ninh Hòa plain, as I have pointed out. The inhabitants of the Annamite villages of the area come and are allowed, during this time, to trade freely with the savages. The latter beat their cymbals during the five days that the fair lasts and exchange products, especially beeswax. "Trương Sấp," the name of this market, signifies, I believe, "exhibition" or "wax market." During the rest of the year the savages fall back under the regulation of the Đò Đưa, the franchised tax collectors who purchase their monopoly for 25 bars of gold a year paid to the citadel, plus a dozen or so bars in bribes (Aymonier, 1886:27-28).

Aymonier refers to these payments indiscriminately as tax and tribute, apparently without recognizing the difference.

No doubt the "savages" who were coming to Ninh Hòa on elephants in troupes of 40 and 50 were Rhade and Jarai from the Darlac plateau (Maitre, 1909:146). According to Maitre this was a regular dry season excursion for many Rhade of the Darlac plateau. This was the same route taken by Yersin when he traveled up into the Darlac plateau area by elephant at the invitation of Me Sao, the Rhade chief of Mdrac (Yersin, 1935:190).

The early French explorers and administrators, without exception, took a very dim view of these commercial agents. They were held to be very exploitative of the highland people and, consequently, responsible for the frequent uprisings in some areas of the highlands (Aymonier, 1885:324-329; Pasquier, 1935a:226-227; Pasquier, 1935b:236). No doubt there was a considerable amount of truth to this charge, particularly in Bình Thuận. Not surprisingly, those nearest the coast with the least chance of escape, were the most severely exploited. Those who lived upon the Darlac plateau, who, because they were less accessible, had greater control over the conditions of contact, were probably not exploited much at all. The agents were abolished by the French in1898 and 1899 (Pasquier, 1935b:236-237; Durand, 1900:285).

Slavery and Slave Trade

Slavery was common among the people of the Southern highlands. In its normal form it was quite mild (Gautier; 1935:55-56). Freedom could be obtained in a number of ways, and slavery served as a means of sanctioning anti-social behavior (Lafont, 1963:146-147; Durand, 1900:307-308). Lafont reported wide and largely disruptive repercussions in social organization when slavery was prohibited among the Jarai because it had been one of the major means of punishing criminals (Lafont, 1963:146-147). However, very early a regional and purely commercial slave trade developed, centering on Cambodia and Laos. In 1641, Von Wusthof, a Dutch trader, reported that slave trade was being carried on with highland people as far east as the Darlac plateau from Sambor, and that, even then, the Chinese were deeply involved in this trade. Slaves represented some of the most important "products" being brought out of the highlands (Maitre, 1912:456).

With the territorial expansion of the Lao during the 18th century and the expansion of Thai hegemony during the third and fourth decades of the 19th century, slave trade became vigorous in the area (Maitre, 1912:482-485; Nyo, 1937:53-54). Phnom Penh and Bangkok were the main centers and Bassac, Khong, and Stung Treng were intermediate centers. Chinese merchants actually controlled the trade (Maitre, 1912:483).

Apparently the more warlike tribes, such as the Sedang and Jarai, were involved in this highly commercialized slave trade, with the result that the whole regions were in virtual anarchy around 1840 (Maitre, 1912:488). The effects of this slave trade upon highland society are best seen through the vignette provided by Me Sao, the despotic Rhade chief from Mdrac. He had, himself, been sold into slavery as a child. Later he was able to control a large number of villages in the Mdrac area by terror. One of the reasons he was so widely feared was because he had alliances with the mandarins in Khánh Hòa to whom he sold enemies whom he captured (Yersin, 1935:190-205).

Lowland Vietnamese were frequently the victims of this slave trade. Apparently the highland people of the Sơn Phòng area frequently raided lowland villages for slaves (Nyo, 1937:53-54, Maitre, 1912: 482, 545-546). The precise degree to which lowland Vietnamese engaged in the slave trade is hard to determine. The observation of Yersin above is a case in point. However, it is clear that they were much less involved than the Lao, Thai, and Cambodians, and, indeed, than the highland people themselves. Maitre claimed that in lowland society slave traffic was very rigidly controlled, those few sales which were made had to be explicitly approved by the civil authorities (Maitre, 1912:494-495). Maitre said:

"From the Cochinchina coast, because of the easy access to the hinterland, the Annamites rapidly entered into relationships with the savages. However, from this side the latter were not as badly treated as in Laos and Cambodia. The relationships between the Annamites and the savages of Cochinchina were primarily commercial; slave raids which became a virtual institution further up along the Mekong never existed in Cochinchina" (Maitre, 1912:494). (My translation)

Disruptive Influences Upon Highland Society

It is very difficult, and perhaps not even wise, to attempt to discuss highland-lowland relationships without making value judgments about the effects these relationships had upon the individuals, groups, and societies concerned. At the same time, at least three value systems impinge upon such judgments, those of the observer, and those of the two societies concerned. Nor can the latter two be considered unitary. Surely the values of the Huế court were not identical to those of the mandarins or those of the convicts banished to the frontiers. The same dissimilarity of values surely applies to highland society. Condominas suggests an inherent value conflict between the matriarchy and male chiefs in Rhade society (Condominas, 1953). Surely the values of the respective highland groups also differed considerably. Thus, there is no obvious set of values one can apply.

It is possible, however, to identify "failures" or "abuses" in terms of departures from ideal models of administration and in terms of conflicts inherent in the contact situation. This I shall do briefly, concerning myself exclusively with abuses visited upon the highland people. Slavery, as an example of an abuse visited upon the lowlanders, has already been mentioned. However, because lowland society was the primary initiating agent in contacts, due to the Nam Tiến and because of lowland society's numeric and political superiority, it seems reasonable to treat it as the subject and highland society as the object. No doubt a more careful analysis of the reciprocal influences the two groups had upon each other would have to modify this approach. French explorers and administrators almost unanimously regarded lowland-highland relationships to be detrimental to the highland people, and sought to limit and control the amount of contact (Aymonier, 1885:324-325; Laborde, 1925:173; Yersin, 1935: 172-173; Pasquier, 1935:226). Maitre did acknowledge that, since they rarely participated in the slave trade, the contact with the lowland Vietnamese was probably not as disruptive as were the contacts with the Thai, Lao, and Cambodians (Maitre, 1912:494-495). The insight of the French critics was not unique, however, because the lowland court was aware of the same abuses to which the colonialists drew attention. In fact, frequent attempts were made to correct them. The method of taxation frequently led to abuses of the highland people. Nguyễn Tấn admitted that there was a relationship between taxation and uprisings in the Sơn Phòng area, and one of his policies in pacifying these people was both to suspend taxes temporarily and to reform the system of taxation. He does not give the details of his reforms.' Nguyễn Cư Trinh was appointed governor of Quảng Ngãi in 1750 with the responsibility of pacifying the belligerent highland people of the Sơn Phòng area. His report to the court in 1751 was that local officials were corrupt, that they were abusing the people, and he proposed that taxation be the responsibility of provincial rather than local officials. He also pointed out that hunters frequented the highland areas and that they mistreated the highland people, causing uprisings. He recommended that no one be allowed to hunt in the highland area without a permit and that anyone who caused the highland people to rebel be prosecuted (DNTL, Vol. 6:215). On several occasions when highland people rebelled, the court suggested that local officials might, in fact, be to blame (DNTL, Vol. 6:112; DNTL, Vol. 16:144-145).

More detail on abuses is provided by the French writers. Not surprisingly, the degree of exploitation seems to have varied inversely with the degree of accessibility of the highland people to the lowland centers. Thus, for example, in Bình Thuận and Khánh Hòa, where some highland people lived quite near the coast, they were occasionally treated as the virtual slaves of local officials (Maitre, 1912:500). At the same time, the Rhade of the Darlac plateau were hardly exploited at all; indeed, the commercial agents who operated in these areas tended to be at the mercy of the highland people.

In a sense, the abuses cited above were petty, mere matters of detail, when compared to the two major ways in which lowland society had a disruptive effect upon highland society. These were loss of land and involvement of highland people in lowland quarrels, frequently leading to severe military repercussions against the highland people. One instance in which highland people became involved in lowland quarrels was during military engagements between Cambodia and Vietnam in the Già Định area.[34] It is notable that in this case, as well as during the Tây Sơn uprising, there is evidence of the use of highland troops in lowland armies. It was said that highland troops were placed at the one flank and Chinese at the other during the early months of the Tây Sơn campaign (Bourotte, 1955:31). These allegations have a very familiar ring to anyone who is familiar with highland-lowland relationships during the 1960's.

There is a very interesting example of the manner in which highland people became implicated in the struggles of the lowland court in Bình Thuận and Khánh Hòa provinces during the middle of the 19th century. This involved an institution referred to as the Hộ Điền Nông, or Hộ Mộ. These were special categories of villages set up by the court of Huế ostensibly to develop new lands. In fact, they, like the military and civilian land development centers before them, had more complicated objectives. The actual purpose of the Hộ Mộ, apparently, was to take care of and facilitate the activities of those who fled the French in Cochinchina, those who were faithful to the nation (nam trung, nghiã sĩ), and to provide intelligence to the Huế court on activities in Cochinchina. This allegation, at least, was made by the French (Aymonier, 1886:14-25; Aymonier, 1885:262-270; 329-333). One technique which they allegedly used to expand their land-holdings was to accuse neighboring villages of controlling lands in excess of those on their civil registers. Considering the state of the civil registers, such accusations were almost

---

[34] Nguyễn Cư Trình, in 1756, came to the aid of 10,000 highland people in the Già Định area who had been forcibly resettled and then abandoned by the Vietnamese general in a campaign against the Cambodians (Auberet, 1863:12-14). The general in question was demoted to the position of a mere company commander (Đội) for having abandoned the highland people.
.

certain to be true. They also attracted villagers away from other villages because they paid no tax and were not required to provide corvee labor. These villages apparently taxed highland people more or less on their own initiative, stole from them, and took away their lands. It was also alleged that they incited highland people to steal buffaloes, themselves eventually benefiting from the legal disputes which resulted. This is only one case in a long history in which the highlands, because they constituted the frontier for lowland society, served as an important battleground of lowland society, and particularly of the lowland court.

Clearing and exploiting new lands was always highly valued by the lowland court, particularly the Nguyễn dynasty. The civilian and military land development villages have already been mentioned (page 20). There is no doubt that large areas now in the hands of lowlanders were originally inhabited by highland people. I have not been able to find evidence that low-landers ever understood or had any appreciation for the highland system of agriculture, not that pressure upon the highland people would necessarily have ceased if they had understood it. It has been noted that the PMTL regarded the highland areas to be "sparsely settled," an attitude which still prevails today (Voth, 1972:60). It is here, more than in any other sphere, where the cultures and their respective economic systems were so profoundly incompatible. It is not an exaggeration to say that the abruptness of the Trường Sơn range and malaria saved the highland cultures and economic systems from virtually complete destruction due to loss of land, a process which would have required incorporation into lowland society upon lowland society's own terms. Now that malaria has been brought under control and the topography no longer inhibits movement as it once did, the manner in which highland society is to be incorporated into the fabric of the nation becomes an open question.

CONCLUSIONS

Several things emerge from this overview of relationships between lowland Vietnamese society and the societies of the Southern highlands. First, surely these relationships played a greater role in Vietnamese history, particularly in the famous Nam Tiến, than has been accorded them in the study of this history to date. Hopefully this is one aspect of Vietnamese history which will receive more attention now that the traditional dynastic historical studies are being replaced by studies concerned with social and economic history. There is no doubt that the Vietnamese frontier was a vibrant, sometimes violent place, demanding the utmost in the innovative capacities of all parties involved in it. Its role in Vietnamese history, when more fully understood, is certain to be significant.

Second, although documentation is far from adequate, there is probably more information available on highland-lowland relationships in Vietnam than for any other country of Southeast Asia. I hope that even this superficial treatment has served to demonstrate that. Thus a special importance attaches to studies of this situation in Vietnam. It is, after all, a general problem throughout the area. All of the countries of Southeast Asia have their equivalent of the highland minorities of South Vietnam and, no doubt, many patterns are similar.

Third, many questions are raised by this discussion which have not been answered. What is the role of the frontier, and, more particularly, of the "barbarians" in lowland Vietnamese culture, literature, politics, etc.?[35] What relationships exist between these patterns in the North during the earlier periods and in the South during the Nguyen dynasty? What were the precise circumstances under which these contacts with southern highlanders first took place? What were the volumes of trade and taxation from region to region? What effect did trade and taxation have upon the highland people? Finally, how must these relationships be regarded in order that the ultimate consequences of their interpretation be humane rather than violent? The new interest in their own history resulting from the autonomy movement since 1958 among the highland people of the Darlac plateau, and the contradicting interpretations of historical individuals and events by Northern and Southern historians is evidence enough that history is never written in a political vacuum. Perspectives not only result from policy, they profoundly influence it. What perspectives, then, should be taken on the minorities question in Vietnam? One of the most important aspects of the problem is how relationships between highland and lowland cultures and societies should be viewed. Are the highland cultures to be viewed as essentially autonomous entities in their own right (Lebar, et al., 1964)? Are they to be regarded as exploited minorities as they were by many of the French commentators, and as they tend to be regarded by Americans who live in the highlands? Or, are they to be regarded as partners in a common historical drama, as is more common, at least rhetorically, in North Vietnam? These are, of course, extremes. The latter appears to be more humane. However, if genuine differences, or genuine exploitative relationships, are overlooked, the results of this apparently humane view will not necessarily be good either. There are limits to how far historical reality can be altered by one's perspective. I hope that this overview will make a contribution to the comprehension of that reality, and that such a comprehension will have humane rather than violent consequences.

---

[35] See Matsumoto, 1959.

BIBLIOGRAPHY

Aubaret, G.
   1863   Histoire et Description de la Basse Cochinchine. Translation of Trang Hoi Duc
           (Trinh Hoai Duc), Gia Định Thống Chí. Paris: Imprimerie Imperiale (Reprinted by
           Gregg International Pdhlishers Ltd., Westmorland, Farnborough, Hants, England,
           in 1969.)

Aymonier, Etienne
   1885   "Notes Sur L'Annam, Premiere Partie: Le Binh Thuan," Excursions et
           Reconnaissances. Saigon: Imprimerie Coloniale (Cochinchine), 24:199-340.
   1886   "Notes Sur L ' Annam: Deuxieme Partie: Le Khanh Hoa, "Excursions et
           Reconnaissances. Saigon: Imprimerie Coloniale (Cochinchine), 27:5-27.
Azemar, H.
   1936   "Les Stieng de Bro'Lam," Varieties Sur Les Pays Mois. Saigon: Le Gouvernement
           de la Cochinchine, pp. 129-165 (Account of an 1886 exploration).

Boudillon, A.
   1915   La Regime de la Propriete Foncier en Indochine. Paris.

Bourotte, Bernard
   1955   "Essai D'Histoire des Populations Montagnards du Sud-Indochinois Jusq'a 1945,"
           Bulletin de la Societe des Etudes Indochinoises, 30:1-99.

Briffaut, Camille
   1912   La Cite Annamite. Paris: Emile Larose (3 Vols.).

Bui Đình
   1963   Đường Len Xứ Thượng. Saigon: Tử Sách Thành Niên Cộng Hóa, Bộ Công Dân
           Vụ.

Buttinger, Joseph
   1956   The Smaller Dragon: A Political History of Vietnam. New York: Praeger.

Cadiere, L.
   1906   "Le Mur de Dong Hoi," Bulletin de l"Ecole Francaise d'Extreme Orient, 6:93:103.

   1912   "Documents Relatifs a 1 'Epoque de Gia Long," Bulletin de l'Ecole Francaise
           d'Extreme Orient, Vol. 7.

Cheon (translator)
    1886   "Bonze et Bonzesse: Dialogue Annamite," Excursions et Reconnaissances. Saigon: Imprimerie Coloniale (Cochinchine), 25:45-98.

Condominas, Georges
    1953   "Introduction au Klei Khan Kdam Yi: Observations Sociologiques Sur Deux Chants Epiques Rhades," Bulletin de l'Ecole Francaise d'Extreme Orient, 47:555-586.

Cotter, Michael
    1968   "Towards a Social History of the Vietnamese Southward Movement ," Journal of Southeast Asian History, 9 (!\larch) : 12-24.

Đại Nam Thực Lục, Tiên Biên va Chính Biên (DNTL)
    1962   Hanoi: Nhà Xuất Bản Sử Học.

Delamarre, Emile
    1924   "La Reforme Communale au Tonkin," La Revue Pacifique, pp. 200-205.

Deloustal, Raymond
    1910   "La Justice dans l'ancien Annam: Traduction et commentaire du Code des Le," Bulletin de l'Ecole Francaise d'Extreme Orient, 10:1-60, 349-392, 461-505.

Dumarest, Andre
    1935   La Formation des Classes en Indochine. Lyon: P. Ferreol.

Durand, E. M.
    1900   "Les Mois du Son Phong ," Bulletin de Geographie Historique et Descriptive, 1:284-322.

Ezzaoui, J.
    1940   "Une version de la legend des deux Sadets," Bulletin de l'Institut Indochinois pour l'Etude de l'Homme, 3:169-174.

Gautier, A.
    1935   "Voyage au pays des Mois: Accompli en Fevrier, Mars, Avril, Mai, et Juin 1882," Varieties Sur Les Pays Mois. Saigon: Governement de la Cochinchine, pp. 31-82.

Gaultier, Marcel
    1935   Ming-Mang. Paris

Goudal, Jean
    1938   Labor Conditions in Indo-China. International Labor Office, Studies and Reports, Series B, No. 26.

Gourou, Pierre
    1940   l'Utilization du Sol en Indochina. Paris: Centre I'Etudes de Politique Etrangere, Travaux des groupes d'etudes.

    1936   Les Paysons du delta Tonkinois: etude de geographie humaine. Paris: Editions d'Art et l'Histoire.

Hammer, Ellen J.
    1954   The Struggle for Indochina. Stanford, CA: Stanford University Press.

Henry, Yves
    1932   Economie agricole de l'Indochine. Hanoi: Imprimerie d'Extrème-orient.

Hoàng Xuân Hãn
    1966   Lý Thường Kiệt - Lịch Sử Ngoại-Giao và Tông-Giao Đời Lý. Saigon: Đại Học Vạn Hạnh.

Jouin, B. Y.
    1951   "Histoire legendaire des deux Sadets," Bulletin de la Societe des Etudes Indochinoises, 26 (1er trimestre).

Jumper, Roy
    1962   Political and Administrative History of Viet Nam. Saigon: Michigan State University Group (Mimeo).

Lã Văn Lo
    1966   "Thử Bàn Về Viết Lịch Sử Các Dân Tộc Thiểu Số Anh Em," Nghiên Cứu Lịch Sử, 91 (October): 39-42.

Laborde, A.
    1925   "La Province de Quang Ngai," Bulletin des Amis de Vieux Hue, pp. 153-192.

Lafont, P. B.
    1963   Toloi Djuat, Coutumier de la Tribu Jorai. Paris: Ecole Francaise d'Extreme Orient.

Lebar, Frank, et al.
    1964   Ethnic Groups of Mainland Southeast Asia. New Haven: Human Relations Area Files Press.

Lê Ngọc Trụ and Phạm Văn Luật
     1961   Nguyễn Cư Trinh với Quyển Sãi Vãi. Saigon. Tân Việt.

Lê Thành Khôi
     1955   Le Viet-nam, Histoire et Civilisation. Paris: Editions de Minuit.

Lương Đức Thiệp
     1971   Xã Hội Việt Nam. Saigon: Hoa Tiên.

Maitre, Henri
     1909   Les Regions Moi du Sud Indochinois: Le Plateau de Darlac. Paris: Librarie Plan,
             Plon-Nourrit et Cie.

     1911   Les Jungles Moi. Paris: Emile Larose.

Matsumoto, Nobuhiro
     1959   "L'Introduction aux etudes Indochinoises (II).

McAlister, John T., Jr.
     1967   "Mountain Minorities and the Viet Minh: A Key to the Indochina War," in Peter
             Kunstadter, Southeast Asian Tribes, Minorities, and Nations. Princeton, New
             Jersey: Princeton university Press, pp. 771- 844.

     1969   Viet Nam: The Origins of a Revolution. New York: Alfred A. Knopf.

Mus, Paul
     1949   "The Role of the Village in Vietnamese Politics," Pacific Affairs, 23:265-272.

     1952   Sociologie d'une Guerre. Paris: Editions du Seuil.

Neiss, Dr. Paul
     1935   "Rapport Sur une Excursion Scientifique Faite chez les Mois l'Arrondissement de
             Baria du 15 Mai au 15 Juin 1880," Varieties Sur Les Pays Mois. Saigon: Le
             Gouvernement de la Cochinchine, pp. 1-30.

Nguyễn Hữu Khang
     1946   La Commune Annamite: Etudes Historiques, Juridiques, et Economiques. Sirey:
             Librarie du Receuil.

Nguyễn Ôn Khê (Nguyễn Tấn)

1904 "Phủ Man Tập Lục, ou Notes Diverses Sur la Region des Moi," Revue Indochinoise, No.7 (1904):445-469, 641-648, 706-716, 789-796. (Abbreviated as PMTL).

Nguyễn Siêu
1960 Phương Đình Dư Địa Chí. (Translated by Nô Mạnh Nghinh) Saigon: Tự Do.

Nguyễn Thiệu Lâu
1950 La Reforme Agraire de 1839 dans le Binh Dinh," Bulletin de l'Ecole Francaise d'Extreme Orient, Vol. 45.

Nguyễn Văn Haù
1969 "Hà Tiên, Chià Khoá Nam Tiến Của Dân Tộc Việt Nam Xướng Đồng Bằng Sông Cửu Lông," Sử Địa, 19-20 (July to December): 260-283.

Nguyễn Văn Thái. and Nguyễn Văn Mùng
1957 A Short History of Vietnam. Saigon: The Times Publishing Company.

Nguyễn Xuân Đạo
1960 "Tổ Chức Hành Chánh Tại Cấp Xã Ở Việt Nam: Khảo Sát Về Những Biến Diễn Trông Lịch Sử, " in Lloyd W. Woodruff and Nguyễn Ngọc Yên, Nghiên Cứu Một Cộng Đồng Thôn Xã Việt Nam: Phần Hoạt Động Hàng Chánh. Saigon: Michigan State Group.

Nghiêm Thẩm
1961 "Tìm Hiểu Đồng Bảo Thượng," Quê Hương, 31:130-150. (I have translated this in Southeast Asia: An International Quarterly, 4(1971):335-364.)

Như Viễn
1965-66 Books 132 to 136 of Khâm Định Đại Nam Hội Điển Sự Lệ. Saigon: Bo Văn Hóa Giao Dục (Compiled originally from 1843 to 1851).

Nouet, L.
1935 "Excursion chez les Mois de la Frontiere Nord-Est du 22 Avril au 9 Mars, 1882," Varieties sur Les Pays Mois. Saigon: Gouvernement de la Cochinchine, pp. 84-103.

Nyo
1936 "La Penetration francaise dans les pays mois, " Bulletin de la Societe des Etudes Indochinoises, 2(1937):45-67 (Proceedings of a conference held in Saigon September 21, 1935).

Pages, M. P.

    1935 "Rapport Sur la penetration en pays moi au cours des cinq dernieres annees, " Varieties Sur les Pays Mois. Saigon: Gouvernement de la Cochinchine, pp. 206-219.

Pasquier, P.

    1935a "Le Resident Superieur en Annam a Messieurs les Residents Chefs de Province en Annam," Varieties Sur les Pays Mois. Saigon: Gouvernement de la Cochinchine, pp. 220-233(Hue, le 30 Juillet, 1923).

    1935b "Annexe a la Circulaire du 30 Juillet, 1923 du Resident Superieur en Annam sur l'organisation de l' interland moi, " Varieties Sur les Pays Mois. Saigon: Gouvernement de la Cochinchine, pp. 235-264.

Phan The Hung

Phan Huy Chu ,

    1960   Lịch Triều Hiến Chương Loại Chí, Tập 1, Dư Địa Chí, Nhân Vật Chí. Hanoi, Nhà Xuất Bản Sử Học.

    1960   Lịch Triều Hiến Chương Loại Chí, Tập 4, Bình Chế Chí, Văn Tịch Chí, Bang Giao Chí. Hanoi, Nhà Xuất Bản Sử Học.

Robequain, Charles

    1929   Le Thanh Hoa: Etude Geographique d'une Province Annamite. 2 Vols. Paris: Universite de Grenoble.

    1944   The Economic Development of French Indochina. New York: Oxford University Press.

Sử Địa

    1970   Special Issue of devoted to the Nam Tiến.

Taboulet

    1955-1956   La Geste Francaise en Indochine (2 Vols.). Paris: Adrien-Maisonnauve.

Trần Trọng Kim

    1965   Việt Nam Sử Lược, 7th Edition. Saigon: Tañ Việt.

United States Department of Agriculture

1951   The Agriculture of French Indochina. Washington, D. C.: U. S. Government
            Printing Office.

Verneville, Huyn de
    1882   "Notice sur la Province de Binh Dinh (Annam), " Excursions et Reconnaissances.
            Saigon: Imprimerie du Gouvernement Cochinchine, No. 11:287-297.

Voth, Donald E.
    1971   "Manipulating the Montagnards," Society, 1972 (Sept.-Oct.): 59-66.

Vũ Văn Hiền
    1939   La Propriete Communale au Tonkin. Paris: Les Presses Modernes.

Wertheim, W. F.
    1966   East-West Parallels: Sociological Approaches to Modern Asia. Chicago:
            Quadrangle Books.

Woodside, Alexander B.
    1972   Vietnam and the Chinese Model. Cambridge: Harvard University Press.

Yersin, Dr.
    1935   "Sept Mois Chez les Mois," Varieties sur Les Pays Mois. Saigon: Gouvernement
            de la Cochinchine, pp. 167-205 (Account of an 1893 expedition).

Printed in the United States
By Bookmasters